# Sweets Without Guilt

## The Fructose Dessert Cookbook

by
Minuha Cannon

The East Woods Press

Library of Congress Cataloging in Publication Data

Cannon, Minuha, 1912-

   Sweets without guilt.

   Includes index.
   1. Cookery (Fructose).  2. Desserts. 3. Confectionery. I. Title
TX819.F78C37      641.8'6      80-18133
ISBN 0-914788-30-2 (pbk.)


Illustrations by Laurie Graybeal.
Photograph of Minuha Cannon courtesy of the Richmond **Independent-Gazette.**
Typography by Raven Type.
Printed in the United States of America by the George Banta Company.

**East Woods Press Books**
Fast & McMillan Publishers, Inc.
820 East Boulevard
Charlotte, NC 28203

# Contents

Foreword by Nancy Bohannon, M.D. ........................ 4

Author's Preface .......................................... 6

Yeasty Sweets ............................................ 9

Cakes .................................................... 24

Toppings and Fillings .................................... 37

Cookies .................................................. 49

Pastries and Foundations ................................ 69

Pie Fillings ............................................. 85

Refrigerator Desserts ................................... 92

Puddings ................................................109

Fruits, Plain and Fancy .................................118

Preserves and Syrups....................................126

Candies and Confections ................................134

Index ...................................................145

Suppliers of Fructose...................................148

About the Author .......................................150

# Foreword

When first invited to write this foreword, I was genuinely delighted that I would once again have the opportunity to write about my favorite sweetener, but I accepted on the condition that the recipes had to be good. After all, I did not want fructose to get a bad name. The recipes in **Sweets Without Guilt** certainly pass that condition. I often tell my patients that you cannot simply substitute fructose for table sugar in grandmother's German chocolate cake recipe, and expect it to turn out well. Frutose is a delightful substance to cook with, as well as metabolically being preferable to table sugar in some people, but it takes either a lot of experience or the following of a good recipe in order to get the good results you deserve.

Personally, I have enjoyed using fructose because it is sweeter than sugar in most uses, so you can use less and save calories. The amount of calories saved depends on its application since it is sweeter in cold uses than in hot applications. It is a flavor heightener and browns beautifully. Therefore, in baking, baking times and temperatures must be carefully followed. Luckily for us, these factors have been taken into account in this book.

As to the other advantages of fructose, I am certain I was asked to write this foreword because of the research I have been doing over the last five years. My interest in fructose was initially spurred because, being a diabetes specialist, I was looking for a good sweetener which could be used safely by diabetics. Before going directly to diabetics, however, I wanted to find out how fructose compared with sucrose (table sugar) in normal people, especially relating to their insulin levels and blood sugar levels. As you know, the most obvious problem in diabetes is elevated blood sugar levels. My initial year of fructose study involved having non-diabetic people drink solutions of 100 grams of either fructose, sucrose, or glucose, each on separate days, and measuring their responses to these sugars. The results of this study were presented at the Annual Meeting of the American Dietetic Association and have subsequently been published in the **Journal of the American Dietetic Association.** These studies showed that fructose caused significantly less rise in the blood sugar levels in the five (5) hours following the drink than did sucrose or glucose, and that much less output of insulin was required. Other hormones were also measured which showed either no difference or less change from the normal levels of the hormones after the fructose as compared to the other two sugars.

Satisfied that fructose appeared to be safe and at least theoretically could have metabolic advantages for some people, the following year was spent studying the effect of these fructose drinks on hypoglycemic individuals. I had already been trying a switch to fructose in people with hypoglycemia (caused by stomach surgery) whom I had seen in my private practice, and was very impressed with the improvement in symptoms. When the results of studies on a group of patients referred by their doctors with the diagnosis of hypoglycemia became available, it again was clear that fructose reduced the rise in blood sugar immediately after the drink, but it also reduced the **fall** in blood sugar that occurred frequently after sucrose or glucose 2½ to 5 hours after the drink. Thus, there was a blunting of blood glucose responses. When the insulin levels were looked at, it became obvious that less insulin had been secreted by these patients after the fructose was taken than after glucose or sucrose, and this reduction in insulin probably explained the **lack** of hypoglycemia after fructose. Indeed, none of the patients had become hypoglycemic after the fructose ingestion. The results of other hormone levels were similar to those found in normal people after the drinks. The results of this study were presented at the Annual Meeting of the American Diabetic Association in June 1978.

The next obvious study was to look at the effect of fructose-containing meals as compared to sucrose-containing meals in diabetics who were unable to make any insulin of their own and who had to receive insulin injections to stay alive. I presented the preliminary results of these studies at an international meeting of diabetes specialists in Hungary in September of 1979. These studies indicate to me that fructose would be an acceptable sweetener for use by diabetics who are not on a severely calorie restricted diet. They showed that the rise in blood glucose after the fructose-containing meal was much less than after the sucrose-containing meals, **despite** the fact that less insulin was given to them before the fructose meal. These studies are still being expanded upon at the Metabolic unit of the University of California in San Francisco.

I must say personally that I am thrilled to see a good dessert cookbook become available using fructose as the sweetener. I am sure many of my child and young-adult diabetic patients will be very glad to have homemade birthday cakes and other treats available, and the rest of us can enjoy the unique and delicious properties of fructose as well!

**Nancy J. Bohannon, M.D.**
Diabetic Specialist
San Francisco, California

# Preface

**Sweets Without Guilt** is an expression of my conviction that good nutrition need not be a form of martyrdom.

Every living cell in the human body needs sugar. Therefore, it is perfectly normal to have a sweet tooth and utterly unreasonable to feel guilty about it. Both **Sweets Without Guilt** and my earlier book, **The Fructose Cookbook**, were inspired by my desire to make our normal, natural fondness for sweets work **for** us instead of **against** us.

Every recipe in this cookbook includes fructose rather than commonly used table sugar.

What is fructose?

It is the sweetest of all natural sugars, found in berries, fruits, vegetables and honey.

Crystalline fructose (100% pure fructose) has four calories per gram, the same number of calories as sugar. The big difference is that fructose is about one-third sweeter than sugar, so less fructose is needed to gain the same sweetening result of sugar. With fructose, you can immediately reduce the amount of sugar in your diet.

Fructose has been shown to satisfy the natural need for sugar without having the hunger-producing effects that ordinary sugar has on many people.

Several sound medical reasons argue for the use of fructose, as Dr. Bohannon has so ably pointed out in her Foreword. Quite apart from medical reasons, fructose actually enhances the flavors and aromas of foods. Desserts with fructose taste better than their sugar counterparts, yet have fewer calories.

In addition, I have found fructose a blessing in the kitchen. It easily dissolves in water and also retains moisture which means baked goods stay fresh longer.

For all these reasons, learning to cook with fructose can be a joyous task.

This second cookbook is devoted entirely to desserts and sweets, customary fare at the end of a meal or between-meal snacks. Most of us love sweets, yet it is difficult to find books emphasizing healthful ingredients for this part of our diet.

Many of these recipes reflect my fondness for traditional and international cuisine as well as the pleasure I take in experimenting with combinations of natural foods. Quite a few were adapted from suggestions of friends. Each one has been approved by at least three tasters other than myself and often as many as twenty.

It is no longer necessary to apologize for the use of ingredients once obtainable only by mail or in health food stores. A growing number of physicians now believe that preventing illness is at least as important as curing it. Because good nutrition is basic to prevention, many health foods can now be found in local supermarkets.

You will notice that a large number of my recipes contain fruit, both fresh and dried. This is inevitable in a fructose cookbook as nothing brings out the flavor of fruit better than fructose. Also, I confess to a strong preference for fruit. When I was a child, my father owned a fruit store, and nothing delighted me more than seeing fascinating new fruits appear with the changing seasons. Much later I lived in Mexico where there are many outstanding native fruits. Our neighbor in Guadalajara grew papayas as large as watermelons.

Produce in general is much tastier and more economical in season. Therefore, I suggest that you use seasonal fruits in the recipes, substituting freely, but making adjustments to variations in sweetness and juiciness.

Although every recipe in this book has been tested and approved precisely as written, I would like to mention ways in which I occasionally vary them when cook-ing for myself.

These recipes frequently use less salt than comparable conventional recipes. For myself, I carry this a step further, often using only a pinch of salt or none at all.

I also keep a variety of healthful foods such as ground seeds, flours, wheat germ and bran on my shelves and often substitute a few tablespoons of these items for equal amounts of white flour in the recipes. I suggest that you let your own needs and tastes guide you.

When testing recipes, I generally oil and sometimes flour the baking pans since this is what most people do. I have found most effective a combination of equal parts of viscous lecithin and oil which I keep in a small jar in my refrigerator. This works not only for greasing baking pans and dishes, but also for sauteing.

Several recipes contain instant coffee to lend a bittersweet flavor to carob and fructose. I use decaffeinated coffee in these recipes; however, the amount is so small compared to other ingredients that instant with caffeine may also be used.

The best kind of peanut butter is the kind you grind yourself. My blender does this without any problem. The next best is the kind which tells you on the label that it contains only peanuts and salt. If you are on a low-salt diet, you should grind your own.

Unless otherwise indicated, ingredients should be at room temperature. If I know I'm going to bake, I take refrigerated ingredients out before breakfast. I put margarine or butter in the oven where the warmth of the pilot light makes them more manageable.

Here are some practical pointers about cooking with fructose.

Because crystalline fructose attracts moisture, it should be stored in tightly-covered containers. If some become damp, let's say in your sugar bowl, this does not particularly harm it — but you must make allowances. Obviously, a teaspoon of fructose which is three-quarters fructose and one-quarter water is not going to be as sweet as a teaspoon of dry fructose, nor will it react the same way in recipes.

The recipes in this book take into account that fructose is more reactive than ordinary sugar. Since it browns more quickly, oven temperatures tend to be lower. When used on top of the stove as in preparing syrups, pickling solutions, jams and jellies, it is important to stir and use a low flame.

Because some people may like to try cooking with the newer liquid fructose on the market, I have adapted some of my recipes to this form. A word of caution: only use 90% liquid fructose in these recipes, as smaller percentages will react differently. I have found 90% liquid fructose to be quite successful, but I would not recommend the purchase of syrup containing smaller percentages of fructose.

I would like to express again my thanks to Robert Aherne who made it all possible from the beginning and to my editors, Sally Hill McMillan and Barbara Campbell for their encouragement and patience in answering many questions. Certainly not least is my gratitude for friends and relatives who have been generous not only with their favorite recipes but also with their understanding of the kinds of vagaries induced by absorption in a creative project.

# Yeasty Sweets

## Pumpkin-Raisin Loaf

½ cup milk
2 tbsps. margarine or butter
½ cup canned pumpkin
¼ cup fructose
½ tsp. salt
½ tsp. cinnamon
¼ tsp. ginger
¼ tsp. nutmeg
¼ tsp. cardamon
¼ cup warm water
  (about 110 degrees)
1 package active dry yeast
1 tbsp. fructose
1 egg, beaten
2 cups unbleached white flour
1 ¼ cups whole wheat flour
  extra flour for kneading
About 2 tbsps. oil for
  greasing dough and loaf
½ cup chopped raisins
⅓ cup sliced almonds

Scald the milk in a large sauce pan. Stir in the shortening, pumpkin, fructose, salt and spices. While this is cooling to lukewarm, add 1 tbsp. fructose and yeast to the warm water and stir. Add the beaten egg to the yeast mixture and pour this in with the sauce pan mixture. Sift together the white and whole wheat flour. Stir 2 cups of this into the sauce pan mixture and beat thoroughly. Stir in the raisins and mix in the rest of the flour, enough to make a dough that leaves the sides of the pan. (This may be a little less or a little more than the specified amount since egg sizes make a difference.) Place on a floured board and knead until smooth, about ten minutes. Place in a well-greased bowl and oil the top and sides of the dough. Cover and put in a warm place to rise until doubled in bulk. Punch down and remove to a well-floured board. Spread and shape into approximately a 9-inch square. Sprinkle evenly with the almond slices and roll up jelly-roll fashion, moistening the end to make it adhere better. Place seam side down in a greased 9-inch by 5-inch by 3-inch loaf pan. Brush the top with oil or melted butter or margarine. Cover and let rise in a warm place until almost doubled. Bake at 375 degrees for about 40 minutes or until the loaf sounds hollow when tapped. This excellent party bread enhances almost any kind of spread, is wonderful with cream cheese and ecstatic with French brie.

## Pumpkin-Raisin Loaf
### adapted to fructose syrup

¼ cup 90% fructose syrup
¼ cup warm water
½ cup milk
2 tbsps. margarine or butter
½ cup canned pumpkin
½ tsp. salt
½ tsp. cinnamon
¼ tsp. ginger
¼ tsp. nutmeg
¼ tsp. cardamon
1 package active dry yeast (1 tbsp.)
1 beaten egg
2 cups unbleached white flour
1½ cups whole wheat flour
extra flour for kneading
½ cup chopped raisins
⅓ cup sliced almonds

In a cup large enough to allow for the growth of yeast, combine 1 tsp. of the fructose syrup with the warm water. In a large sauce pan scald the milk. Stir in the shortening until melted. Remove from heat and mix in the remaining fructose, pumpkin, salt and spices. Let cool to lukewarm. Meanwhile, add the yeast to the warm water. When the sauce pan mixture is about 110 degrees, comfortably warm for your little finger, stir in the warm water and yeast mixture. Mix in the beaten egg. Sift together the white and whole wheat flours. Stir 2 cups of this into the sauce pan mixture. Stir in raisins and add rest of flour, enough to make a soft but firm dough. Continue with the kneading to the final baking as directed in preceding recipe.

## Raisin Bread Toffee

4 slices raisin bread
½ cup finely chopped nuts
½ tsp. nutmeg, optional
1 cup fructose
1 tbsp. margarine or butter

Cut each slice of bread into 9 pieces. This is done by cutting into 3 equal strips, (2 cuts), then cutting each strip into 3 equal pieces. To save time, you can pile the bread slices together, make 2 cuts in one direction and 2 more cuts at right angles. Mix the chopped nuts with nutmeg, if used. Heat the fructose in a small, heavy skillet until melted. Add the margarine and continue heating until bubbly and golden. Turn off heat and place about 6 of the bread cubes into the skillet, turning with a fork until evenly coated. Roll one at a time into the chopped nuts covering all sides. It will probably be necessary to re-heat the caramelized sugar briefly a couple of times before all the cubes are coated. Let cool before serving. These store well in an air-tight container. Makes 36 pieces.

## Potato Coffee Cake (Kartoffel Kuchen)

This is an adaptation of an old Dutch recipe and conjures a vision of a thrifty Dutch housewife who knew what to do with leftover mashed potatoes.

¼ cup margarine or butter
1 cup water in which potatoes have been cooked
½ cup fructose
1 egg
1 tbsp. yeast granules
1 tbsp. fructose
1 cup whole wheat flour
2½ cups unbleached white flour
1 tsp. salt
1 tsp. cinnamon
½ tsp. nutmeg
½ cup mashed potatoes
1 cup jam or marmalade
1 recipe streusel topping

In a large sauce pan heat the potato water to lukewarm. Pour ½ cup of this into a small glass. Add the margarine and the ½ cup of this into a small glass. Add the margarine and the ½ cup fructose to the water remaining in the sauce pan and heat until margarine melts. Stir the yeast granules and 1 tbsp. fructose into the potato water in the glass. Allow the sauce pan mixture to cool to lukewarm. Stir in the yeast mixture and beat in the egg. Sift together the whole wheat flour, white flour, salt, cinnamon and nutmeg. Add the mashed potatoes to the sauce pan mix·ture and gradually beat in the dry ingredients to make a firm dough. Turn onto a well-floured board and knead for about 10 minutes. Place in a greased bowl and rotate so that all sides are oiled. Cover and let rise in a warm place until double in bulk. Remove from bowl and, shaping to fit, place in 10-inch square baking pan. Let rise until double in bulk. Spread lightly with the jam of marmalade and sprinkle the streusel evenly over the entire coffee cake. Bake at 375 degrees 30 to 40 minutes until nicely browned.

Yeasty Sweets

13

## Multi-Grain Sweet Roll Dough

This very pliable dough is one of my favorites because it is not only excellent nutritionally, but it can be used for coffee cakes. Millet gives it a nutty texture.

1 cup milk
⅓ cup millet
¼ cup margarine or butter
½ cup fructose
¾ tsp. salt
¼ cup water, lukewarm
1 tbsp. dry yeast
1 egg
1½ cups rye flour
1½ cups whole wheat flour
½ cup white flour, unbleached
½ cup bran

In a large sauce pan heat the milk, millet and shortening until the shortening is melted. Stir the dry yeast into the lukewarm water. Stir the fructose and salt into the sauce pan mixture. Let cool to lukewarm. Beat the egg into the sauce pan mixture and stir in the yeast and warm water mixture. Sift together the rye, wheat and white flours. Combine with the bran and beat these ingredients into the sauce pan mixture. Enough flour should be added to make a soft dough that can be handled with floured hands. Knead for 10 minutes on a well-floured board. Place in a greased bowl, brush with oil and cover. Let rise in a warm place until doubled. Shape and bake as directed in individual recipes. This dough may be refrigerated.

## Almond and Raisin Upside Down Snails

½ recipe Multi-Grain Sweet Roll Dough
3 tbsps. fructose
1 tsp. cinnamon
½ cup chopped raisins
2 tbsps. vegetable oil, about
14 tsps. melted margarine or butter
14 tsps. fructose
7 tsps. sliced almonds

On a well-floured board roll out the dough to form an oblong 8 inches by 14 inches. Combine the fructose and cinnamon and sprinkle over the dough. Spread the raisins evenly over the dough and roll up the long side to form a 14-inch roll pressing closely. Place 1 tsp. each of melted margarine or butter and fructose in 14 muffin tins. Spread ½ tsp. sliced almonds evenly over the combined margarine and fructose. Cut the roll of dough into 14 one-inch snails. Flatten each snail slightly between you palms and place in a muffin tin cut side up. Brush the tops with vegetable oil and let stand for 1 hour. Bake at 375 degrees for 20 to 30 minutes. Let stand for 10 minutes. Loosen the snails with a spatula and invert over aluminum foil. If some of the almond and fructose base remains in the muffin tin, remove it with a spatula and spread on the snails. Makes 14 snails.

## Cream Cheese Filled Crescents

¼ recipe Multi-Grain Sweet Roll Dough (see recipe)
½ cup cream cheese
2 tbsps. lemon juice
3 tbsps. fructose
2 tsps. cornstarch
1 tbsp. melted butter

Mix thoroughly the cream cheese, lemon juice, fructose and cornstarch. Roll the dough out very thin. Cut into 3-inch circles. On the center of each circle place a rounded teaspoon of the cream cheese mixture. Fold the circle over to form a half moon shape and press the edges tightly together. Pull the ends gently to make a crescent shape. Brush with melted butter and let stand in a warm place for ½ hour. Bake at 375 degrees 15 to 20 minutes. Makes about 20 crescents.

## Yeast Dough Cinnamon Cookies

½ recipe Multi-Grain Sweet Roll Dough (see recipe)
2 tbsps. melted margarine or butter
3 tbsps. fructose
1 tsp. cinnamon
marmalade, or cranberry glaze, optional

On a well-floured board roll out the dough very thin, using about ¼ at a time. Cut cookies with cookie cutters and place on well-greased sheets. Brush with melted butter or margarine. Mix thoroughly the cinnamon and fructose. Sprinkle this on top the buttered cookies. Small touches of marmalade or glaze can be used to give color and taste variety. The amount depends on the size of the cookies. I use about ¼ tsp., for example, for a star-shaped cookie; perhaps ½ tsp. for a reindeer. Let stand in a warm place for 1 hour, then bake at 375 degrees 10 to 15 minutes until lightly browned. Makes about 3 dozen cookies, varying depending on the size of your cookie cutters.

## Refrigerator Sweet Roll Dough

This relatively simple dough adapts itself to many uses, plus you can use as much as you want and store the rest in the refrigerator.

3½ cups white unbleached flour
1 cup whole wheat flour
1 tbsp. yeast
1 cup milk
⅓ cup margarine
¾ tsp. salt
½ cup fructose
1 egg

Combine the yeast with 2 cups of the flour. Heat the milk and margarine together just until margarine is melted. Stir in fructose and salt. Cool until lukewarm, about 115 degrees. Add the yeast and flour mixture and beat thoroughly. Beat in the egg. Add the rest of the flour, enough to make a soft but firm dough. Turn onto a board and knead. Place in a greased bowl turning so that the dough is greased on all sides. At this point, if you wish, you may place the dough in an expandable plastic bag (it rises a little in the refrigerator) and store in the refrigerator up to 3 days. Or you may use some of it, perhaps ½, and store the rest, or you may want to use all of it immediately. In the latter case, cover the greased bowl with the dough in it and place in a warm spot until double in bulk. Punch down and shape as desired. Brush the tops with melted butter. Let rise again and bake at 400 degrees for 15 to 20 minutes.

## Refrigerator Sweet Roll Dough
## adapted to fructose syrup

3½ cups white unbleached flour
1 cup whole wheat flour
1 tbsp. dry yeast
1 cup milk
⅓ cup margarine or butter
¾ tsp. salt
⅓ cup 90% fructose syrup
1 egg

Combine the yeast with 2 cups white flour. Heat together the milk and shortening just until the shortening is melted. Stir in fructose syrup and salt. Let cool to lukewarm. Add the yeast and flour mixture and beat thoroughly. Beat in the egg. Mix in the rest of the flour, enough to make a soft but firm dough. Continue with the kneading, etc., as directed in preceding recipe.

## Cheese and Raisin Topped Coffee Cake

½ recipe Refrigerator Sweet Roll Dough
   (see recipe)
1 cup dry curd cottage cheese
1 egg
¼ cup fructose
2 tsps. flour
2 tbsps. lemon juice
1 tsp. grated lemon rind
¼ cup chopped raisins
¼ cup flavored yogurt
¼ cup sliced almonds

Roll the dough out into a 10-inch circle or 7-inch by 11-inch oblong depending on whether you use a 9-inch-round baking dish or a 6-inch by 10-inch baking dish. Press into the sides and bottom of the baking dish. Beat together the cottage cheese, egg, fructose, flour, lemon juice and rind and raisins. Spread the flavored yogurt on the dough and spoon the cheese mixture evenly over this. Sprinkle the sliced almonds evenly over the top. Let stand in a warm place for 1 hour. Bake in a 400 degree oven for ½ hour. This is very good served warm, and you may wish to time your baking with this in mind. It can be re-heated. Makes about 12 servings.

# Crescents

My first introduction to crescents and how to make them came from the wife of a Norwegian doctor in Madison, Wisconsin who also introduced me to refrigerator dough.

To make one dozen crescents take one half the Refrigerator Sweet Roll Dough (see recipe) after it has risen and been punched down. Shape into a round disc and place on a well-floured board. Roll out into a circle 11 inches in diameter. Cut into 12 pie-shaped pieces. Spread with filling of your choice and roll up starting from the rim of the circle. This is excellent filled with Mocha-Milk Topping (see recipe); also good spread with a tablespoon of jam, jelly or marmalade on each crescent; or simply sprinkled with cinnamon and sugar; or thinly spread with one of the Flavored Yogurts (see recipes). Brush with melted butter and let rise in a warm place until almost doubled. Bake at 400 degrees for 15 to 20 minutes.

## Little Brown Babas

This is a chocolate-tasting variation of the traditional French Savarins or Baba au Rhum.

¼ cup lukewarm water
1 tbsp. active dry yeast
1 tbsp. fructose
⅓ cup milk
3 tbsps. soft butter or margarine
2 eggs
⅓ cup fructose
1 cup unbleached white flour
½ cup whole wheat flour
½ cup powdered carob
1 tsp. powdered coffee

Place the lukewarm water, yeast and 1 tbsp. fructose in a cup. Heat the shortening and milk together stirring until the shortening is melted. Let cool to lukewarm. Beat in the eggs and ⅓ cup fructose. Stir in the softened yeast mixture. Sift together the remaining ingredients and combine with the liquid mixture. Beat thoroughly. Cover with a damp cloth and place in a warm spot for one hour. Push one rounded tablespoonful into each of greased muffin tins. Place in a warm spot and cover again with a damp cloth. Let rise until almost doubled. Bake at 350 degrees until a toothpick comes out clean, about 20 to 30 minutes. This makes about 20 babas.

They can be served plain or pricked with a fork and hot syrup poured over them as with traditional rum babas. They may also be frosted or glazed. This dough may also be baked in a tube pan to make a cake in which case it should be baked about 40 minutes. The cake may also be pricked and soaked with hot syrup or frosted or glazed.

## Oatmeal-Buttermilk Sweet Dough

1 cup warm water
½ cup fructose
1 tbsp. active dry yeast
2 cups oatmeal
1 cup buttermilk
2 tbsps. salad oil
3 cups unbleached white flour
1 tbsp. salt
½ tsp. ground anise seed (optional)

Place the warm water with 2 tbsps. of the fructose and the yeast in a bowl. Stir. Add the oatmeal, buttermilk, and salad oil and mix thoroughly. Sift together the remaining fructose, flour, salt and anise seed, if used. Beat this in about a cup at a time using enough flour to make a smooth dough that will leave the sides of the bowl. Turn onto a well-floured board and knead for ten minutes. Place in a greased bowl and turn the dough so that it is entirely covered with oil. Cover with a cloth that has been slightly dampened in warm water and let rise in a warm place until doubled in bulk. Punch down and shape as directed in individual recipes. Part or all of this dough can be stored in the refrigerator for several days. To store, oil and place in a plastic bag that will allow for some expansion. Makes enough for 2 coffee cakes or loaves.

## Hearty Prune-Nut Bread

1 cup moist-pack prunes, pits removed
½ cup chopped nuts
2 tsps. lemon rind
¼ tsp. nutmeg
1 tbsp. lemon juice
½ recipe Oatmeal-Buttermilk Sweet Dough
3 tbsps. fructose
1 tsp. cinnamon

Combine thoroughly the first five ingredients. After punching down the oatmeal-buttermilk sweet dough, roll it out to form an 8-inch square. Combine the fructose and cinnamon and sprinkle it evenly over the rolled-out dough. Distribute the prune mixture evenly on top of this. Roll the dough up, tucking the prunes in as you go along, to form a cylindrical loaf. Moisten the edge to form a firm closure. Place seam side down in an 8-inch by 4-inch by 3-inch high greased loaf tin. Oil the top and let rise in a warm place until almost doubled. Bake at 375 degrees for 50 minutes. This is good served hot or toasted with butter or cream cheese. Or shred some cheddar on top of slices and bake until the cheese melts.

## Yeasty Date-Sunflower Seed Bars

¼ recipe sweet yeast dough
2 tsps. melted butter
1 cup chopped dates
¼ cup water
¼ cup fructose
1 tbsp. lemon juice
⅓ cup shelled sunflower seeds
1 recipe Versatile Coconut Topping or any of the
   recipes for streusel toppings

Roll the yeast dough (I like the Oatmeal Buttermilk Sweet Dough recipe for this) out thin to fit a greased 10-inch square baking tin. Brush with melted butter and note the time. The prepared pan of bars should go into the oven 1 hour from this time. In a small saucepan bring to a boil the dates, water and fructose. Cook until thick but spreadable, about 5 minutes. Remove from heat and stir in the lemon juice and sunflower seeds. Spread the date mixture on top of the yeast dough. Distribute streusel or topping evenly over this. Let stand until 1 hour has passed from the time you fitted the yeast dough into the baking pan. Bake at 350 degrees for ½ hour. Cut into squares or bars. Makes about 3 dozen bars, depending on the size you like them to be.

# Cakes

## Apple-Date Cake

½ cup whole wheat flour
½ cup white flour
⅓ cup fructose
1 tsp. cinnamon
¼ tsp. salt
3 tbsps. margarine
½ cup chopped apple
2 tbsps. chopped dates
½ tsp. baking soda
1 egg
¾ cup yogurt
1 tsp. vanilla

Combine the first 5 ingredients. Cut margarine into this mixture until crumbly. Save 6 tbsps. for topping. Add chopped apple, dates and baking soda to the remainder. Mix thoroughly. Beat together the egg, yogurt and vanilla. Combine thoroughly with the first mixture. Spread into a 9-inch round dish, greased. Sprinkle with reserved topping. Bake at 375 degrees until toothpick comes out clean, about 30 minutes. Makes 8 servings.

## Apple-Date Cake
## adapted to fructose syrup

3 tbsps. margarine or butter
¼ cup 90% fructose syrup
½ cup plus 2 tbsps.
   whole wheat flour
½ cup unbleached white flour
1 tsp. cinnamon
¼ tsp. salt
½ cup chopped apple
2 tbsps. chopped dates
½ tsp. baking soda
1 egg
¾ cup yogurt
1 tsp. vanilla

In a sauce pan large enough to hold all ingredients, melt the shortening. Remove from heat and stir in the fructose syrup. Sift together ½ cup of the whole wheat flour, the white flour, cinnamon and salt. Stir this into the sauce pan mixture. In a small bowl place the remaining 2 tbsps. whole wheat flour and 6 tbsps. of the sauce pan mixture. Blend these together and place in the refrigerator. Stir chopped apple, chopped dates and baking soda into sauce pan mixture. Beat together the egg, yogurt and vanilla. Pour into the sauce pan and beat thoroughly. Spread into a greased 9″ round dish. Remove the small bowl mixture from the refrigerator and, crumbling between your fingers, sprinkle the contents over the top of the cake. Bake at 350 degrees 30 to 40 minutes until nicely browned and a toothpick inserted comes out clean.

Cakes

**25**

## Apple-Ginger Upside Down Cake

3 tbsps. melted margarine
⅓ cup fructose
1 tsp. cinnamon
2 cups sliced apples
¼ cup raisins (optional)
¼ cup margarine
½ cup fructose
1 egg
1 cup flour, unbleached
1½ tsps. baking soda
1/8 tsp. salt
2 tsps. ginger
⅔ cup buttermilk

Place the melted margarine in a 9-inch round by 2-inch deep baking dish. Combine the cinnamon and ⅓ cup fructose. Stir one half of this mixture into the margarine. Lay the sliced apples evenly over this and sprinkle the remaining fructose and cinnamon over the apples. Sprinkle the raisins over this. Cream together ½ cup fructose and ¼ cup margarine. Add egg and beat. Sift together the flour, baking soda, salt and ginger. Add alternately in about 4 portions with the buttermilk beating well after each addition. Spoon this batter evenly over the apples. Bake at 350 degrees about 40 minutes, until a toothpick comes out clean and cake is nicely browned.

## Pineapple Upside Down Cake

Follow the above recipe with these exceptions: Omit the cinnamon. Add the entire ⅓ cup fructose to the 3 tbsps. margarine. Lay slices of pineapple in a pattern over this. If you wish, ½ seedless date may be placed in center of each slice. Continue with batter and baking as above.

## Margaret's Apple-Nut Torte

1 egg
⅓ cup fructose
½ tsp. vanilla
1/8 tsp. salt
½ cup unbleached white flour
½ tsp. baking powder
⅔ cup chopped apples
⅓ cup chopped nuts,
    or hulled sunflower seeds

Beat the egg. Add the fructose and vanilla and beat again thoroughly. Sift together the salt, flour and baking powder. Add to the first mixture and beat thoroughly. Add the chopped apples and nuts, or sunflower seeds, and mix well. Spread in an 8-inch cake tin. Bake at 350 degrees about ½ hour until lightly browned and an inserted toothpick comes out clean. This is good served either with yogurt, whipped cream or ice cream.

## Banana Yogurt Cake

½ cup margarine or butter
¾ cup fructose
2 eggs
¾ cup yogurt
¼ cup orange juice
1 cup mashed banana
1 cup whole wheat flour
1 cup white flour
1 tsp. baking powder
½ tsp. baking soda
¼ tsp. salt

Cream the margarine and fructose. Beat in the eggs one at a time. Combine the yogurt, banana and orange juice. Sift together the remaining ingredients. Add the liquid ingredients alternately with the dry ingredients in about 4 parts beating after each addition. Turn into a 10-inch square greased and floured pan and bake at 325 degrees until a toothpick comes out clean, about 1 hour. Makes 25 two-inch square servings.

Cakes

**27**

## Banana Yogurt Cake
### adapted to fructose syrup

½ cup 90% fructose syrup
½ cup margarine or butter
2 eggs
¾ cup yogurt
¼ cup orange juice
1 cup mashed banana
1 cup whole wheat flour
1 cup white flour
1 tsp. baking powder
½ tsp. baking soda
¼ tsp. salt

Heat together the fructose syrup and margarine or butter, just until the shortening is melted. Let cool slightly. Beat together the eggs, banana, yogurt and orange juice. Sift together remaining ingredients. Add dry ingredients alternately with moist ingredients to the fructose syrup and margarine mixture in about 4 stages, beating well after each addition. Bake as directed in preceding recipe.

This is good served plain, but for company you might like some of the toppings. I like it with Orange Custard as a topping. Makes 25 two-inch square servings.

## Caramel Cake

¼ cup margarine or butter
½ cup fructose
1 egg, separated
½ tsp. maple flavoring
⅓ cup Caramelized Fructose Syrup (see recipe)
⅓ cup buttermilk
1/8 tsp. salt
1 tsp. baking soda
1 cup unbleached white flour

Cream together the shortening and fructose. Beat in the egg yolk and maple flavoring. Combine the buttermilk and syrup. Sift together the salt, baking soda and flour. Add these dry and moist ingredients alternately in 3 stages. Beat thoroughly. Beat the egg white until it holds peaks. Fold into the batter. Turn this into an 8-inch round, greased and floured cake tin. Bake at 325 degrees for ½ hour. Double the recipe if you would like a layer cake.

## Carrot and Pineapple Cake

2 cups whole wheat flour
½ tsp. salt
1½ tsps. baking soda
1 tsp. ground cloves
1 cup vegetable oil
1¼ cups fructose
3 eggs
1 tsp. vanilla
½ cup yogurt
1½ cups grated carrots
½ cup drained unsweetened crushed pineapples

Sift together the flour, salt, soda and cloves. Cream the vegetable oil and fructose. Add the eggs one at a time, beating well after each addition. Beat in the vanilla and portions of the yogurt alternately with the sifted dry ingredients. Stir in the carrots and crushed pineapple, mixing thoroughly. Spread in a 12-inch by 7-inch by 2-inch baking dish and bake at 350 degrees. If you are using the Pineapple Glaze (see recipe) which is very good with this cake, bake for 30 minutes, spread with glaze and bake about 15 minutes more. If you wish a plain cake or are planning to use the Cream Cheese Frosting (see recipe) bake approximately 45 minutes.

## Old Dutch Spice Cake

3 tbsps. margarine
¾ cup fructose
1 egg
2 cups sifted flour
1 tsp. baking powder
1 tsp. baking soda
1/8 tsp. salt
1 tsp. crushed anise seeds
½ tsp. nutmeg
½ tsp. allspice
½ tsp. ground cloves
½ tsp. cinnamon
1½ cups buttermilk

Cream together margarine and fructose. Beat in the egg. Sift together the dry ingredients and add alternately with the buttermilk in four stages beating thoroughly after each addition. Pour into a greased 9-inch tube pan and bake at 325 degrees for about one hour. Invert and frost. Broiled frostings (see recipes) are good with this cake. Frost while hot.

## Strawberry Shortcake

4 cups strawberries
⅓ cup fructose
3 cups unbleached white flour
3 tsps. baking powder
2 tbsps. fructose
½ tsp. salt
⅓ cup shortening
2 eggs
½ cup milk
1 cup whipping cream
1 tsp. vanilla
2 tsps. melted butter

Clean strawberries, remove stems and crush. Stir in the ⅓ cup fructose. Sift together the flour, baking powder, salt and 2 tbsps. fructose. Cut the shortening in with a pastry blender or two knives. Beat together the eggs and milk. Pour into the sifted dry ingredients and mix to form a soft dough. Divide in two equal parts. Knead one part lightly and roll into a 9-inch circle. Place in a greased cake tin. Brush top with melted butter. Repeat with the second half of dough and place the second circle on top the first one. Bake at 425 degrees approximately 20 minutes. Separate into 2 layers. Whip the cream and stir in vanilla. Top one layer with ½ the cream. Spread with ½ the sweetened strawberries. Place the second layer on top the first and repeat with the whipped cream and strawberries. Makes approximately 8 servings.

## Orange Gelatin Cake

⅓ cup vegetable oil
½ cup fructose
3 eggs
1 cup unbleached white flour
1 cup whole wheat flour
¼ tsp. salt
1 tsp. baking soda
½ cup sour milk or buttermilk
1 envelope gelatin
¼ cup cold water
¼ cup boiling hot water
¼ cup orange juice
¼ cup grated orange rind
1 recipe Orange Syrup

Cream together the oil and fructose. Add the eggs one at a time beating well between additions. Sift together the flours, salt and baking soda. Add ⅓ of these dry ingredients to the first mixture and beat thoroughly. Add the rest alternately with the sour milk in two stages, beating well after each addition. Combine the gelatin and cold water. Stir in the hot water until the gelatin is dissolved. Add to the mixture in the bowl and beat well. Beat in the orange juice and orange rind. Spread in a greased and floured baking dish approximately 12 inches by 7 inches and 2 inches deep. Bake at 350 degrees 30 to 40 minutes until nicely browned and a toothpick comes out clean. While still hot, prick all over with a fork and spread evenly with Orange Syrup (see recipe). Let cool before slicing. Makes between 12 and 18 servings.

## Cheese Cake with Marmalade

1 unbaked pie crust
½ cup marmalade or preserves
3 eggs, separated
⅔ cup fructose
juice and rind of one small, or ½ medium lemon
½ cup milk
1 pound dry curd cheese
½ tsp. salt
2 tbsps. flour
½ cup Flavored Yogurt (see recipes)

Put the unbaked pie crust in a 400-degree oven for 5 minutes. I like the Shredded Wheat and Peanut Crust recipe for this. Remove and spread with ½ cup marmalade or preserves. In a bowl beat the egg yolks and fructose. Add the lemon juice and rind, milk, cheese, salt and flour. Beat until thoroughly blended. Beat the egg whites until they hold their shape. Fold into the cheese mixture. Pour over the marmalade in the pie crust. Bake in a 350-degree oven for ½ hour. Remove from oven and spread with yogurt flavored with the same kind of marmalade as used with the crust. Return to oven and bake for another half hour until knife inserted comes out clean. Makes 1 nine-inch cake, enough for 10 to 12 servings.

## Plum Swirl Cheese Cake

3 eggs, separated
¼ cup fructose
1½ cups ricotta cheese
1 tsp. vanilla
½ cup Plum Jam (see recipe)

Beat egg yolks with fructose. Stir in the ricotta cheese and vanilla, mixing thoroughly. Beat egg whites until stiff but not dry. Fold into the cheese mixture. Pour into an unbaked pie crust of your choice. I like Crumbly Ginger Foundation or Coconut Cookie Crust (see recipes) with this cheese cake. Spread the plum jam on top of this in a swirled pattern and cut into the cheese cake as you would for a marble cake. Place in a 400-degree oven and reduce heat to 325 degrees. Bake about 50 minutes, until knife comes out clean.

## Peanut-Pumpkin Cake

2 tbsps. melted margarine
½ cup fructose
1 egg
½ cup canned pumpkin
1 tbsp. lemon juice or
   apple cider vinegar
⅔ cup whole wheat flour
2 tbsps. wheat germ
1 tsp. baking soda
¼ tsp. ginger
¼ tsp. ground cloves
½ cup chopped peanuts
3 tbsps. Caramelized Fructose
   (see recipe)

Cream the margarine and fructose. Beat in the egg, canned pumpkin and lemon juice or apple cider vinegar. Sift together the flour, wheat germ, baking soda, ginger and ground cloves. Add to the batter and beat until thoroughly mixed. Fold in ¼ cup of the chopped peanuts and spread in a baking dish 6-inch by 9-inch by 2-inch. Sprinkle the remaining ¼ cup chopped peanuts evenly over the cake and press in lightly. Spoon the Caramelized Fructose Syrup over the top, turning the baking dish slightly from side to side to help it spread evenly. Bake at 350 degrees 40 to 50 minutes until nicely browned and a toothpick comes out clean. This can be served either plain or with whipped cream and makes about 15 servings.

Cakes

33

## Corn Meal Ginger Cake

¾ cup corn meal
¾ cup whole wheat flour
1 tsp. soda
¼ tsp. salt
2 tsps. ginger
¼ tsp. nutmeg (optional)
2 tbsps. melted butter or margarine
½ cup fructose
1 egg
2 tsps. grated orange rind
1 cup sour milk or buttermilk

Sift together the first 6 ingredients. Cream the fructose into the melted shortening. Add the egg and orange rind and mix well. Add the dry ingredients and the sour milk or buttermilk in three stages, beating well after each addition. Turn into a 9-inch round cake tin and bake at 325 degrees for 45 minutes. 6 to 8 servings. Orange Custard (see recipe) makes a good topping.

## Zucchini-Carob Cake

¼ cup margarine or butter
¾ cup fructose
2 eggs, separated
1 tsp. vanilla
1½ cups chopped zucchini
¼ cup buttermilk
1 cup white flour
½ cup whole wheat flour
¼ cup powdered carob
1 tsp. baking soda
¼ tsp. ground nutmeg
¼ tsp. ground cloves

Cream together the fructose and margarine. Beat in the egg yolks and vanilla. Combine the buttermilk with the chopped zucchini and beat into the first mixture. Sift together the remaining dry ingredients and beat in with the moist ingredients. Beat the egg whites until stiff. Fold into the batter. Pour the batter into a greased and floured 7-inch by 11-inch pan or ovenware glass dish. Bake at 325 degrees for 45 minutes until a toothpick comes out clean. This has a moist almost pudding texture and is good served plain. For a special occasion, frost with Creamy Orange Broiled Frosting (see recipe) topped with coconut.

## Angelita Cupcakes

¾ cup fructose
¼ tsp. salt
1 tsp. baking powder
1 cup flour
1 tsp. vanilla
½ cup milk
3 egg whites

Sift together the first four ingredients. Add the milk and vanilla and beat until smooth. Beat the egg whites until they hold soft peaks. Fold into the batter until just blended. Place 2 tablespoons of this into each cupcake tin. (My 2 tablespoon coffee measure works very well for this.) Bake at 350 degrees for 15 minutes. Invert cupcake tins until cool. Remove with spatula. Makes about 20 cupcakes.

## Tipsy Little Angels

If you are in a festive mood, you may like to prick the cupcakes with a fork and pour about 2 tablespoons of your favorite liqueur over each cupcake. It is good with various syrups, too.

## Scottish Tea Scones

½ cup vegetable oil
2 eggs
¼ cup milk
2 cups unbleached white flour
½ tsp. salt
2 tsps. fructose
1 egg white

Stir together the oil, 2 whole eggs and milk. Sift together the flour, salt, baking powder and 1 tbsp. of the fructose. Make a well in these dry ingredients and pour the first mixture into it. Working from the sides of the bowl towards the center mix until you have a soft dough. Place on a well-floured board and knead for about 2 minutes. Roll to form an oblong about ½-inch thick, 6 inches wide and 10 inches long. Beat the egg white lightly. Brush onto the top of the oblong and sprinkle with the remaining 1 tbsp. fructose. Cut into diamond shapes. Bake at 425 degrees about 15 to 20 minutes until nicely browned. These are best served hot with butter and jam. Makes about 1 dozen scones.

## Samovar Tea Cakes

2 eggs plus 1 egg yolk
1 tbsp. fructose
1½ cups flour
½ tsp. salt
¾ tsp. baking powder
1 egg white
2 tbsps. fructose

Beat the eggs, egg yolk and 1 tbsp. fructose with an electric mixer or vigorously by hand until light. Sift together the flour, salt and baking powder. Add the dry ingredients to the egg mixture and beat thoroughly to make a soft but firm dough. Turn onto a floured board and knead for 1 minute. Roll out into an oblong 5 inches by 9 inches. Brush egg white over the entire top of the dough. You won't need all the egg white for this; save the rest for an omelet. Sprinkle the 2 tbsps. of fructose over the egg white. With a sharp knife cut the oblong crosswise into 9 one-inch pieces. Cut each piece in half making 18 in all. Bake on a greased cookie tin at 425 degrees for about ½ hour. Makes about 18 tea cakes.

These are also good with 2 tbsps. sesame or poppy seeds added to the dough.

# Toppings
# and Fillings

## Creamy Boiled Frosting

1 cup fructose
1/8 tsp. cream of tartar
¼ cup cold water
1 egg white
1 tsp. vanilla

Combine the fructose, cream of tartar and water in a sauce pan and cook until it reaches about 245 degrees on the candy thermometer, somewhat above the soft-ball stage but not as high as the hard-ball stage. While this is cooking, beat the egg white stiff. Continue the beating as you slowly pour the syrup into the egg white. Add vanilla. Continue beating until the frosting is cool and proper consistency for spreading. This will cover a 10-inch round or an 11-inch by 7-inch cake comfortably and a 9-inch round cake with enough left over to pass spoons to the children. It should be made shortly before serving the cake as fructose does attract moisture and the frosting will become softer as time goes by. However, it can be prepared and frozen.

## Creamy Orange Boiled Frosting

Substitute 3 tbsps. orange juice and 1 tbsp. lemon juice for ¼ cup water in the above recipe.

## Pretty Pink Frosting

Substitute ¼ cup cranberry juice for the ¼ cup water in the above recipe.

## Broiled Caramel Frosting

3 tbsps. soft margarine or butter
1 tbsp. milk
1 cup fructose

Combine all ingredients in a small sauce pan and heat, stirring constantly, just until margarine is melted and ingredients are well-mixed. Spread over hot cake, sweet bread or cookies and place under the broiler. Watching carefully to avoid burning, let broil until it begins to sizzle. This is enough to glaze a 9-inch round cake.


## Broiled Coconut-Caramel Frosting

Follow above recipe adding ½ cup grated coconut.


## Broiled Caramel-Nut Frosting

Follow recipe for broiled caramel frosting adding ½ cup chopped or sliced nuts.

## Versatile Coconut Topping

This simple baked-on frosting adds a glamorous note to cookie bars, pies, cakes or coffee cakes.

¼ cup fructose
1 tbsp. unbleached white flour
1 egg
2 tbsps. lemon juice
1 cup shredded coconut

Sift together the fructose and flour. In a small bowl beat the egg and lemon juice. Stir in the fructose and flour mixture. Add the coconut and mix thoroughly. Spread evenly on unbaked cake or cookie dough or pie. If the cake takes much longer than ½ hour, as is the case with some coffee cakes, spread on the cake for the last half hour. Enough to top a 10-inch square pan of bar cookies, or a 9-inch round pie or cake.

## Cream Cheese Frostings

These are traditional with Carrot Cake (see recipe) but are also excellent with any kind of fruit cake or cookie bars, also delicious simply spread on toast. I usually use Neufchatel cheese, which is 20% lower in calories than ordinary cream cheese.

### I

1 cup cream cheese
¼ cup softened margarine or butter
¼ cup fructose
1 tsp. vanilla

Cream the above ingredients together thoroughly. Spread just before serving. Store leftovers in refrigerator. Enough to frost one 12-inch by 7-inch cake.

### II

1 cup cream cheese
2 tbsps. softened margarine or butter
¼ cup fructose

Cream together thoroughly the cheese and softened margarine or butter. In a heavy skillet heat the fructose until melted and golden brown. Turn off heat and stir the cheese mixture into this until blended. Spread on cake while still hot. This is also best made just before serving. Leftovers should be refrigerated. Makes one 12-inch by 7-inch cake.

Toppings and Fillings

## Orange Custard

½ cup fructose
2 tbsps. cornstarch
2 tbsps. flour
1/8 tsp. salt
¾ cup boiling water
2 egg yolks
⅓ cup orange juice
2 tbsps. grated orange rind
1 tbsp. lime or lemon juice
1 tbsp. butter or margarine

In the top of a double boiler combine the first five ingredients. Cook directly over low heat. Stirring constantly, bring to a boil. Continue cooking over hot water, stirring occasionally, until thick. Beat the egg yolks. Add the orange and lemon juice and the grated orange rind to the egg yolk and stir. A tablespoon at a time, add about 4 tbsps. of the thickened mixture to the egg and orange juice mixture, stirring after each addition. Pour back into the top of the double boiler and add butter. Cook directly over very low heat until thick. Do not let it boil. This is a very good cake topping.

**Orange Custard**
**adapted to fructose syrup**

2 tbsps. corn starch
2 tbsps. flour
1/8 tsp. salt
¾ cup boiling water
⅓ cup 90% fructose syrup
2 egg yolks
⅓ cup orange juice
2 tbsps. grated orange rind
1 tbsp. lime or lemon juice
1 tbsp. butter or margarine

In the top of a double boiler combine the corn starch, flour and salt. Stir in the boiling water and syrup. Bring this mixture just to a boil, cooking directly over low heat and stirring constantly. Continue cooking over hot water until thick, stirring occasionally. Continue, following the above recipe's directions, beginning with the beating of the egg yolks.

**Orange Custard Pie**

To make an orange custard pie, double the above recipe and pour into a baked pie shell. Top with a meringue (see recipe).

## Cottage Cheese Topping or Filling

1 tbsp. melted margarine or butter
3 tbsps. fructose
1 egg
½ tsp. vanilla
1 tbsp. flour
⅔ cup small curd cottage cheese

Cream together the shortening and fructose. Beat in the egg and vanilla. Stir in the flour and cottage cheese. Beat until creamy. Use as topping on unbaked coffee cakes and bake as directed. This is used in the recipe for Marbled Cottage Cheese Brownies and is also excellent as filling for cheese tarts, using unbaked pastry in cupcake tins and baking for about 45 minutes at 350 degrees.

## Mocha-Milk Topping

2 tbsps. melted margarine
¼ cup fructose
6 tbsps. powdered carob
¾ cup skimmed milk powder
½ tsp. instant decaffeinated coffee powder
¼ cup water

Stir together the fructose, carob, milk powder and coffee powder. Mix thoroughly with the melted margarine. Add enough water to make a spreadable consistency and mix thoroughly. Spread on top of unbaked cake or cookies or use as filling in sweet rolls. Bake as directed.

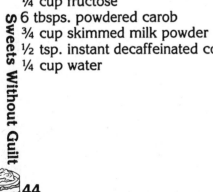

## Oatmeal Streusel Topping

½ cup fructose
6 tbsps. oatmeal
¼ cup flour, whole wheat or unbleached white
¼ tsp. salt
3 tbsps. margarine or butter

Combine the fructose, oatmeal, flour and salt in a bowl. Cut the margarine or butter into this mixture and work with fingers until crumbly. Sprinkle on top of coffee cake, or pie, etc. and bake as directed.


## Whole Wheat Streusel Topping

½ cup whole wheat flour
⅓ cup fructose
1/8 tsp. salt
½ tsp. nutmeg or other spice to taste
¼ cup margarine or butter

Combine the flour, fructose, salt and spice in a small bowl. Cut the margarine or butter into this to form a crumbly mixture. Sprinkly over cake or pie evenly. Bake until lightly browned at 400 degrees, 20 minutes to ½ hour.

Toppings and Fillings

## Whole Wheat Streusel Topping
### adapted to fructose syrup

2 tbsps. margarine
2 tbsps. 90% fructose syrup
6 tbsps. flour
1/8 tsp. salt
¼ tsp. nutmeg or other spices to taste

It is a good idea to make this ahead of time, as it needs to be refrigerated for easier handling. Melt the margarine in a small sauce pan. Stir in the fructose syrup. Let cool. Mix together the remaining ingredients and stir into the margarine and syrup mixture. Refrigerate for at least a half-hour. Crumbling between your fingers, sprinkle over dough or pie filling and bake as directed in the preceding recipe.

## Cheese and Whole Wheat Streusel Topping

Add ¼ cup grated cheddar or swiss cheese to the above recipe and bake as directed.

## Cranberry Glaze

The pretty color of this glaze adds visual appeal to puddings or anything else you choose to top with it. It is especially appropriate for holidays.

1 tsp. cornstarch
¼ cup fructose
¼ cup water
½ cup cranberries

In a small sauce pan stir together the fructose and cornstarch. Add the water and heat, stirring, until the fructose is dissolved. Add the cranberries and cook until all the cranberries have popped. This can be spread on baked puddings and baked during the last 15 minutes of the baking time. Makes ½ cup of glaze.

## Orange-Spread Glaze

2 tbsps. margarine or butter
2 tbsps. fructose
3 tbsps. orange juice

Melt the margarine or butter in a small sauce pan or skillet. Add the fructose and orange juice. Cook until syrupy. Makes enough to top one coffee cake or two dozen small rolls.

This is excellent on yeast dough coffee cakes or rolls to be spread on top the dough after shaping and before final rising. The shortening in this topping seals the moisture in the dough and, therefore, prevents it from drying out while rising.

## Lemon-Spread Glaze

In the above recipe substitute lemon juice for orange juice and increase the fructose to 3 tbsps.

## Pineapple Glaze

¼ cup fructose
1 tbsp. cornstarch
½ cup pineapple juice
1 cup unsweetened crushed pineapple
½ cup grated coconut, optional

Stir together the fructose and cornstarch in a small sauce pan. Stir in the pineapple juice and bring to a boil stirring continuously. Add the crushed pineapple and grated coconut if used, and bring to a boil. Cook to desired thickness. If it is going to be baked, as with Carrot Pineapple Cake (see recipe), it can be thinner, since the continued baking will thicken it.

## Meringue Topping

3 egg whites
¼ tsp. cream of tartar
5 tbsps. fructose
½ tsp. vanilla, optional

Egg whites should be at room temperature or slightly warmer. I put them in my oven, which is warmed by the pilot light, for about ½ hour. Beat the egg whites for about 1 minute. Add cream of tartar and continue beating until stiff. Add the fructose very slowly and continue beating. Stir in vanilla, if used. Pile on top of pie, spreading to the very edges to seal in the filling. Bake as directed.

# Cookies

## Anise Banana Bars

1 cup mashed bananas
1 tbsp. anise seed
½ cup margarine or butter
½ cup fructose
1 egg
1 tsp. vanilla
1 cup unbleached white flour
½ cup whole wheat flour
2 tsps. baking powder
1/8 tsp. salt

Combine the anise seed with the bananas and set aside. Cream the margarine or butter with the fructose. Beat in the egg and vanilla. Add the mashed bananas with anise seed and combine thoroughly. Sift the dry ingredients into the mix-ture and beat until well-mixed. Spread in a 10-inch square pan and bake at 325 degrees for 45 minutes or until a toothpick comes out clean. Makes 30 to 50 cookies, depending on how big you like them.

## Banana-Date Oatmeal Squares

1 cup oatmeal, uncooked
1 cup whole wheat flour
½ tsp. soda
¼ tsp. salt
¼ tsp. ground cloves
¼ tsp. ground allspice
¼ cup margarine or butter
¼ cup fructose
1 egg
1 cup mashed banana
½ cup sliced dates
¼ cup sliced almonds
1 tsp. vanilla

Sift together the flour, soda, salt and spices and stir into the oatmeal. Cream the margarine with the fructose and beat in the egg. Stir in the dates, almonds and vanilla into the mashed banana. Add this to the creamed mixture and stir until well-mixed. Add the dry ingredients and beat thoroughly. Turn into a greased 10-inch square pan and spread evenly. Bake at 350 degrees for ½ hour or until toothpick comes out clean. Makes 3 dozen squares.

## Old-Fashion Peanut Butter Cookies, modified

½ cup peanut butter
¼ cup butter or margarine
½ cup fructose
1 egg
1 tsp. vanilla
½ cup unbleached white flour
¾ cup whole wheat flour
1 tsp. baking powder

Cream together the peanut butter, margarine and fructose. Mix thoroughly with the egg and vanilla. Sift together the flours and baking powder and add to the first mixture in three parts blending thoroughly after each addition. Refrigerate for easier handling. Shape into walnut-sized balls and place on cookie sheet two inches apart. Press the balls with the points of a fork to make the traditional texture. Bake at 350 degrees until golden brown, about 15 minutes.

## Peanut Butter Bars

The above dough may be pressed, without prior refrigeration, into a 7-inch by 12-inch or 9-inch square baking dish. Bake until golden brown, about 20 minutes. Allow to cool before slicing. Makes between 3 and 4 dozen cookies.

## Peanut Butter Jam-wich Cookies

1 cup whole wheat flour
1½ cups oatmeal, uncooked
½ cup fructose
¼ cup margarine or butter
½ cup crunchy old-fashioned peanut butter
1 egg
½ cup berrypicker's spiced preserves
(or any other fructose jam)

Stir together in a bowl the whole wheat flour, oatmeal and fructose. Cut into this with a pastry blender the margarine and peanut butter. Save out ⅔ cup of this mixture for topping. Add 1 egg to the remainder in the bowl and mix thoroughly. Spread this mixture in a greased 10-inch by 7-inch pan. Over this spread evenly the preserves or jam. Sprinkle the topping you have saved over the preserves. Bake at 375 degrees 40 to 45 minutes. Cool before slicing into bars. Makes 32 cookies.

## Potato-Carob Brownies

⅓ cup margarine
½ cup fructose
1 egg
1 tsp. vanilla
½ cup mashed potato
⅓ cup unbleached white flour
½ cup whole wheat flour
¼ cup powdered carob
1 tsp. instant coffee
½ cup chopped nuts

Cream together the fructose and the margarine. Beat in consecutively the egg, vanilla and mashed potato. Sift together the white flour, whole wheat flour, carob and coffee. Beat these ingredients into the first mixture. Add the nuts and mix thoroughly. Spread into a greased 10-inch by 6-inch baking dish and bake at 375 degrees for about 40 minutes until an inserted knife comes out clean. Makes about 2 dozen brownies.

Cookies

## Shredded Wheat and Raisin Cookies

3 tbsps. margarine or butter
½ cup fructose
1 egg
2 tbsps. unflavored yogurt
½ cup whole wheat flour
¼ tsp. salt
½ tsp. baking soda
½ tsp. cinnamon
½ tsp. ground cloves
1 cup shredded wheat crumbs
⅓ cup chopped raisins
½ cup Mexican Raisin Nuggets (see recipe)

Cream together the fructose and margarine. Beat in the egg and yogurt. Sift together the flour, salt, baking soda and spices. Beat sifted ingredients thoroughly into the first mixture. Add the shredded wheat crumbs, raisins and sliced candy. Mix thoroughly. These can be baked either as dropped cookies or bars. For dropped cookies, place rounded tsps. 2 inches apart on a greased cookie sheet. Bake at 350 degrees about 20 minutes. For bars, spread in a greased 10-inch by 6-inch baking dish and bake approximately ½ hour. Makes about 2 dozen cookies.

## Shredded Wheat and Raisin Cookies
## adapted to fructose syrup

3 tbsps. margarine or butter
½ cup 90% fructose syrup
1 egg
1 tbsp. unflavored yogurt
¾ cup whole wheat flour
¼ tsp. salt
½ tsp. baking soda
½ tsp. cinnamon
½ tsp. ground cloves
1 cup shredded wheat crumbs
⅓ cup chopped raisins
½ cup Mexican Raisin Nuggets (see recipe) sliced
    1/8-inch thin

Heat together the shortening and fructose syrup in a large sauce pan until shortening is melted. Let cool to lukewarm. In the meantime you can sift together the dry ingredients, prepare the wheat crumbs and slice the Raisin Nuggets. Beat the egg and yogurt into the saucepan mixture. Add the sifted dry ingredients and mix thoroughly and beat again. Add the remaining ingredients. These can be baked either as dropped cookies or as bars following the directions in the above recipe. Makes about 2½ dozen cookies.

## Mocha Brownies

¼ cup margarine or butter
½ cup fructose
2 eggs
1 tsp. vanilla
½ cup unbleached white flour
¼ cup whole wheat flour
⅓ cup powdered carob
1 tsp. coffee powder

Cream together the shortening and fructose. Beat in the eggs and vanilla. Sift together the remaining ingredients and beat into the first mixture until well-blended. Turn into a greased and floured 8-inch square tin. Bake at 350 degrees 30 to 40 minutes. Makes about 16 brownies.

## Cottage Cheese Brownies

Prepare the above batter. Spread about one-half of it in a greased and floured 9-inch square baking dish. Over this spread evenly 1 recipe of Cottage Cheese Topping or Filling (see recipe). Spoon remaining Mocha Brownie Batter evenly over the filling. Using a dull knife, make cuts to produce a marbled effect. Bake in a 350-degree oven for 35 to 40 minutes. Makes about 2 dozen brownies.

## Delectable Beet Bars

2 tbsps. vegetable oil
⅓ cup fructose
1 egg
⅓ cup mashed banana
¼ cup small curd cottage cheese
⅔ cup grated beets
¼ cup chopped nuts
1 tbsp. grated orange peel
2 tbsps. orange juice
¼ cup chopped dates or raisins
¼ cup whole wheat flour
1 tsp. cinnamon
1 tsp. ground cloves
2 tbsps. bran
⅓ cup oatmeal
½ tsp. baking soda

Cream together the oil and fructose. Beat in the egg. In a separate bowl mix together the banana, cheese, beets, nuts, orange peel, orange juice and dried fruit. Sift together the flour, spices and baking soda. Stir into these dry ingredients the bran and oatmeal. Add these last two mixtures in alternating portions to the first mixture, beating well after each addition. Bake in a greased and floured 10-inch by 6-inch pan or dish at 325 degrees for about 1 hour. Cool and cut into bars. Makes about 2 dozen cookies.

These bars, chock full of healthful ingredients, are also very tasty. For an extra melt-away effect, try them topped with Cream Cheese Frosting (see recipe).

## Festive Almond Cookies

½ cup whole wheat flour
½ cup unbleached white flour
1/8 tsp. salt
1 tsp. baking powder
⅓ cup margarine or butter
⅓ cup fructose
3 egg yolks
½ tsp. almond flavoring
½ cup sliced almonds
About 2 tbsps. cubed dates,
    or marmalade or raisins

Sift together the flours, salt and baking powder. Cream well the shortening and fructose. Beat in the egg yolks and almond flavoring. Add the sliced almonds and beat until well mixed. Refrigerate dough for easier handling. Form into 1-inch balls and place an inch apart on lightly greased baking sheet. Dates should be cut in ¼-inch cubes. Press one cube into each cookie, or one raisin if raisins are used. If using marmalade, press each cookie with little finger or end of chopstick and fill with 1/8 tsp. marmalade. Red pepper marmalade adds a festive color to the cookie. Bake at 300 degrees for 30 minutes. Makes 30 cookies.

## Puffed Cereal Carob Cookies

½ cup whole wheat flour
¼ cup unbleached white flour
⅓ cup carob powder
¼ tsp. cinnamon
¼ tsp. nutmeg
¼ tsp. ground cloves
1 tsp. baking powder
¼ cup margarine
⅓ cup fructose
1 egg
¼ cup milk
½ cup puffed cereal
    (wheat, rice)

Sift together the first 7 ingredients. Cream the margarine with the fructose until well-blended. Beat in the egg. Add ½ the dry mixture and half the milk, beating thoroughly. Add the remainder with the puffed cereal and beat until well-blended. Push rounded teaspoonfuls onto a greased cookie sheet 1 inch apart. Bake at 350 degrees for about 20 minutes. Makes about 2½ dozen cookies.

## Lemon-Glazed Peanut Butter Bars

1 recipe Peanut Butter Bars (see recipe)
½ cup fructose
3 tbsps. white, unbleached flour
2 eggs
3 tbsps. lemon juice

Bake the peanut butter bars as directed, but just 10 minutes. Stir the fructose and flour together. Beat the lemon juice into the eggs. Combine both mixtures and beat until well-blenced. Remove the Peanut Butter Bars from the oven and pour the lemon mixture over them, tilting the pan so that the dough is covered evenly. Return to oven and continue baking at 350 degrees for 15 to 20 minutes.

## Date and Peanut Butter Clusters

½ cup flour
¼ tsp. baking soda
1/8 tsp. salt
3 tbsps. coconut, grated
¼ cup pitted dates
1 tsp. flour
2 tbsps. margarine
¼ cup peanut butter
¼ cup fructose
1 egg
1 tsp. vanilla

Sift together the flour, baking soda and salt. Spread the 1 tsp. flour on a small bowl and cut the dates into it in small pieces. Stir the floured dates and the coconut into the dry mixture. Cream together the margarine, peanut butter and fructose. Add the egg and vanilla, and beat well. Add the dry mixture and beat until well-blended. Drop by rounded teaspoons on a lightly greased cookie sheet. Bake 15 to 20 minutes at 350 degrees until golden brown. Makes about 20 cookies. If you're expecting a crowd, double or triple recipe.

# Date-Nut Pumpkin Cookies

¼ cup margarine
⅓ cup fructose
1 egg
¾ cup canned pumpkin
¼ tsp. salt
¼ tsp. cinnamon
¼ tsp. ginger
¼ tsp. allspice
1 cup white unbleached flour
⅓ cup whole wheat flour
2 tsps. baking powder
½ cup chopped dates
½ cup chopped nuts

Cream together the margarine and fructose. Beat in the egg and pumpkin. Sift together the salt, spices, flour and baking powder. Add to the first mixture and beat until thoroughly blended. Stir in the nuts and dates. Push well-rounded teaspoons of this onto a lightly greased baking tin. Flatten just a little. Bake at 375 degrees 20 to 25 minutes until golden brown. Makes about 30 cookies.

## Gertrude Maynard's Wholesome Tasty Cookies

½ cup margarine or butter
1 cup fructose
2 eggs
1 cup whole wheat flour
1 cup oatmeal
2 tbsps. skimmed milk powder
1 tsp. baking powder
½ tsp. salt
1 tsp. cinnamon
2 cups grated carrots
2 tsps. vanilla
1 cup chopped fruit
1 cup chopped nuts or seeds

Cream together the shortening and fructose. Beat in the eggs. Sift together the flour, milk powder, baking powder, salt and cinnamon. Mix this with the oatmeal and add to the first mixture. Beat thoroughly. Add grated carrots and vanilla and again beat thoroughly. Thus far the mixture makes about 3 cups of thick batter. If you like variety, you may wish at this point to divide the batter in equal portions and add ½ cup each of nuts and fruit to each one. For example, you might add ½ cup chopped apples and ½ cup sunflower seeds to one portion, and ½ cup chopped dates and ½ cup chopped almonds to the other. Other combinations are raisins and sesame seeds, or pears and walnuts. Or, you may prefer to use the whole batter and stir in a full cup of fruit and a full cup of nuts or seeds. Place heaping teaspoons onto a greased cookie tin and flatten slightly. Bake at 350 degrees until lightly browned, about 25 minutes. Makes about 4 dozen cookies.

## Gertrude Maynard's Wholesome Tasty Cookies adapted to fructose syrup

½ cup 90% fructose syrup
¼ cup butter or margarine
1 egg
1½ tsps. vanilla
¾ cup whole wheat flour
1 tbsp. skimmed milk powder
¾ tsp. baking powder
¼ tsp. salt
¾ tsp. cinnamon
1 cup grated carrots
¾ cup oatmeal
½ cup chopped fruit
½ cup chopped nuts

In a large sauce pan heat the fructose syrup and shortening just until shortening is melted. Let cool. Beat in egg and vanilla. Sift together flour, milk powder, baking powder, salt and cinnamon, and beat the sifted ingredients into the sauce pan mixture. Add the carrots, oatmeal, fruit and nuts, and mix thoroughly. Drop by rounded teaspoons onto a greased cookie sheet and flatten slightly. Bake at 350 degrees until lightly browned, 25 to 30 minutes. Store in a tight container. Makes about 30 cookies.

## Filo Cookies

This is an excellent way to use Greek filo dough which you have inadvertently allowed to become too dry for other uses. In fact, after tasting these cookies, you may find yourself purposely letting the dough dry out.

1 cup filo, broken into coarse crumbs
1 tbsp. margarine or butter
2 eggs
¼ cup fructose
¼ cup whole wheat flour
2 tbsps. bran
½ cup tender-dried apricots, sliced
½ cup diced candied orange peel
2 tbsps. lemon juice

Heat shortening and filo crumbs together in a skillet until crumbs are lightly browned, and set aside. Beat the eggs and fructose together until light. In a small bowl, combine apricot slices and orange peel with lemon juice and set aside. Beat the whole wheat flour and bran into the egg-fructose mixture. Add the filo and fruit mixtures and stir thoroughly. Drop by rounded teaspoons on a greased cookie sheet about 1½ inches apart. Bake at 375 degrees until golden brown, 10 to 15 minutes. Makes about 2 dozen cookies.

## Oatmeal Lace Cookies

½ cup margarine, softened
⅓ cup fructose
1 egg
½ tsp. vanilla
¼ cup flour
1/8 tsp. salt
¾ cup oatmeal

Cream together the margarine and fructose. Beat in the egg and vanilla. Sift together the salt and flour and stir into the mixture. Add the oatmeal and beat thoroughly. Push from a rounded half tsp. onto a lightly greased cookie tin and flatten with the back of a spoon or spatula. These should be an inch apart. You will see that as the cookie tin is re-used, it is not necessary to grease it again. Bake at 350 degrees until brown around the edges, about 10 minutes. Let cool for 1 minute before removing with a spatula. Makes approximately 3 dozen cookies.

## Oatmeal Lace Cookies adapted to fructose syrup

⅓ cup 90% fructose syrup
½ cup margarine
1 egg
½ tsp. vanilla
⅓ cup flour
1/8 tsp. salt
1 cup oatmeal

In a medium-sized sauce pan, large enough to hold the entire batter, heat together the syrup and margarine until the margarine is melted. Let cool. Beat in egg and vanilla. Sift together the flour and salt. Combine with the oatmeal. Add these dry ingredients to the sauce pan mixture and beat thoroughly. Continue and bake as directed above. Makes about 4 dozen.

## Coconut Lace Cookies

Follow the above recipe, substituting 6 tsps. grated unsweetened coconut and 6 tbsps. oatmeal for the ¾ cup oatmeal.

## Chewy Carob Wafers

This recipe is for people who wish to avoid eggs.

½ cup fructose
¼ cup margarine or butter
¼ tsp. almond extract
½ cup flour
pinch of salt
2 tbsps. powdered carob
1 tsp. instant coffee powder

Heat the fructose in a small, heavy sauce pan just until it melts. Stir in the shortening and almond extract. Add the remaining ingredients and mix thoroughly. Take a small amount in your fingers as soon as it is cool enough to handle and form into a ball about 1 inch in diameter. Flatten in the palm of your hand to form a circle 2 inches in diameter and place on lightly greased cookie sheet. Continue with the rest of the dough, working quickly. If the dough should become too stiff to handle, place the sauce pan over hot water until it is workable. Bake at 375 degrees about 10 minutes. Makes approximately 20 cookies.

## Nut and Rye Wafer Marguerites

2 egg whites at room temperature
⅔ cup fructose
½ cup finely chopped nuts
½ cup rye cracker crumbs (any unsweetened
   cracker or bread crumbs may also be used)
½ tsp. vanilla

Place the fructose in a small heavy pan and heat over low flame until completely melted and beginning to bubble. Meanwhile beat the egg whites until they form soft mounds when lifted. If I use an electric beater, they will be ready slightly before the fructose is melted. As you continue beating the egg whites, add the hot melted fructose **very** slowly. Fold in the nuts, crumbs and vanilla. Push by rounded tablespoonfuls onto a cookie sheet which has been greased with a combination of equal amounts of lecithin and salad oil. (My favorite non-stick mixture.) Bake at 250 degrees 30 to 40 minutes until lightly browned. Keep in turned-off oven until cool. Store in an air-tight container. Makes about 2 dozen Marguerites.

## Nut and Rye Wafer Marguerites
## adapted to fructose syrup

½ cup 90% fructose syrup
2 egg whites
½ cup finely chopped nuts
½ cup rye cracker crumbs
½ tsp. vanilla

Bring the fructose syrup to a boil and let simmer for 5 minutes. Meanwhile beat the egg whites until they form soft mounds when lifted. Continue beating the egg whites and add the heated syrup very slowly. Fold in the nuts, crumbs and vanilla. Bake as directed in above recipe.

## Open Sesame Yam Gems

¼ cup margarine or butter
½ cup fructose
1 egg
2 tbsps. buttermilk or sour milk
½ cup mashed cooked yams
1 cup whole wheat flour
½ tsp. ginger
¼ tsp. nutmeg
⅓ cup unbleached white flour
2 tbsps. bran
2 tbsps. wheat germ
½ tsp. salt
½ tsp. baking soda
⅓ cup currants
2 tbsps. sesame seeds

Cream together the shortening and fructose. Beat the egg and combine thoroughly with buttermilk and yams. Combine these mixtures and beat thoroughly. Sift together the flours, spices, salt and baking soda. Stir in the bran, wheat germ, currants and sesame seeds. Add to the first mixture in 4 stages beating thoroughly after each addition. Drop from rounded tsps. onto a greased cookie sheet. Flatten slightly. Bake at 350 degrees about 20 minutes until nicely browned. Store in covered container. Makes about 2 dozen cookies.

## Carrot-Coconut Cookies

4 tbsps. salad oil
⅔ cup fructose
2 eggs
⅔ cup mashed cooked carrots
1 cup unbleached white flour
½ cup whole wheat flour
½ tsp. salt
1 tsp. baking powder
1 tsp. cinnamon
3 tbsps. wheat germ
½ cup chopped raisins
¼ cup shredded coconut

Cream together the oil and fructose. Add eggs and carrots and beat well. Sift together the flours, salt, baking powder and cinnamon. Stir the wheat germ, raisins and coconut into the sifted ingredients. Add to the moist ingredients in four stages, beating well after each addition. Drop by rounded tsps. onto a greased cookie sheet and flatten each cookie with the back of a spoon until it is about ¼-inch high. Bake at 350 degrees until nicely browned, about 20 minutes. Makes about 2 dozen cookies.

# Cream Cheese Rolled Cookies

2 tbsps. melted margarine or butter
¼ cup Neufchatel cheese
2 tsps. lemon juice
1/8 tsp. almond extract
¼ cup fructose
1 egg
1 cup and 2 tbsps. white unbleached flour
½ tsp. baking powder
¼ tsp. salt
¼ tsp. baking soda

Stir together the shortening, cheese, lemon juice and almond extract. Beat in the fructose until creamy. Add the egg and beat thoroughly. Sift together 1 cup of flour and the remaining ingredients. Beat thoroughly into the first mixture. Whether or not you need the remaining 2 tbsps. of flour depends on the size of the egg. The dough should be thick and sticky, not stiff. Refrigerate for ease of handling. Roll out very thin and cut with cookie cutters. These make nice holiday cookies. If you wish to make them more colorful, spread a little Sweet Ball Pepper and Lime Marmalade (see recipe) on the cookies, or Cranberry Glaze (see recipe). Bake at 375 degrees 8 to 10 minutes.

# Pastries and Foundations

## Cheese Pastry

⅓ cup grated cheese, cheddar or Swiss
1 cup whole wheat flour
1 tbsp. wheat germ
2 tbsps. fructose
1/8 tsp. salt
⅓ cup melted margarine or butter
2 tbsps. hot water

In a 9-inch pie tin stir together the cheese, flour, wheat germ, fructose and salt. Stir in the melted margarine and hot water and knead until well mixed. Press this dough into the sides and bottom of the pie tin. Bake at 425 degrees for 20 minutes for a baked pie shell, or bake according to the directions given with the pie filling you are using.

## Cheese Triangles

⅓ cup feta cheese
⅓ cup small curd cottage cheese
2 tbsps. fructose
¼ tsp. cinnamon
¼ tsp. ground cloves
3 sheets filo pastry
3 tbsps. melted butter
syrup (optional)

Mix thoroughly the cheeses, fructose and spices. Cut the filo into 2-inch wide strips and pile them on each other to prevent drying. You may find it necessary to lay a damp paper towel over the strips you are not immediately using. Dab a strip with butter the whole length. Place a teaspoon of the cheese mixture at one end. Fold a top corner over this to the opposite side making a triangle. Continue folding, going from side to side and keeping the triangle shape until you have used the entire length of the pastry. Repeat this process with each of the strips until you have used up the cheese mixture and strips. Bake at 350 degrees for about ½ hour. If you wish, you can lay these close together on a plate and pour your favorite syrup over them. They are also delicious plain. Makes about 20 triangles.

## Almond-Coconut Crust

3 tbsps. margarine or butter
½ cup sliced almonds
1 cup flaked coconut
2 tbsps. fructose

Melt the margarine or butter in a pie tin. Mix thoroughly the almonds, coconut and fructose. Stir into the melted shortening. Press against the bottom and sides of the pie tin. Chill until firm. For a filling that needs to be baked, spoon the filling into the crust in the pie tin and bake as directed. With a filling that does not need to be baked, place the pie tin with crust in a 350 degree oven and bake until lightly browned, 10 to 15 minutes.

## Almond-Coconut Crust
## adapted to fructose syrup

4 tsps. 90% fructose syrup
3 tbsps. margarine or butter, melted
½ cup sliced almonds
1 cup flaked coconut

Stir the fructose syrup and melted shortening together in a pie tin. Mix thoroughly the almonds and coconut and stir into the syrup and shortening mixture. Continue, following the directions above.

## Coconut Cookie Crust

3 tbsps. melted butter or margarine
¼ cup fructose
1 egg yolk
½ cup whole wheat flour
¼ tsp. salt
2 tbsps. bran
1 tbsp. wheat germ
½ cup grated coconut
2 tbsps. water, approximately

Cream together the shortening and fructose. Blend in the egg yolk. Combine the flour, salt, bran wheat germ and coconut and mix thoroughly with the first mixture to make a crumbly dough. Add just enough water so that you can form a cohesive ball. Wrap this in plastic or foil and chill in refrigerator for about an hour. Press into bottom and sides of pie dish. For a baked pie shell bake at 400 degrees until golden brown, about 15 to 20 minutes. Makes 1 bottom pie crust.

Pastries and Foundations

**71**

## Crumbly Ginger Foundation

A tasty bottom for custard fillings or fruits with custards poured over them.

¼ cup margarine
2 tbsps. fructose
½ tsp. ginger
1 ¼ cups flour, whole wheat or unbleached white,
   as you prefer

Cream together the margarine and fructose. Mix the ginger with the flour. Cut this mixture into the margarine and fructose until crumbly. Press into the bottom and sides of a 9-inch round cake tin or ovenproof dish. Bake at 375 degrees for 5 minutes, if used with a filling that will be baked. If the filling will not be baked, bake this foundation for 15 minutes or until lightly browned.

## Crumbly Ginger Foundation adapted to fructose syrup

¼ cup margarine
5 tsps. 90% fructose syrup
½ tsp. ginger
1 ¼ cups flour, whole wheat or unbleached white
   as you prefer

Melt the margarine. (Since this recipe takes little time to complete, I simply set my oven at 375 and put the margarine in a pie dish in the oven until melted. Leaving the oven on will bring it up to 375 degrees in approximately the time it takes to complete the preparation.) Stir the fructose syrup into the margarine. Sift the flour and ginger into the combined margarine and fructose syrup. Mix well. (This will be less crumbly than the above recipe; nevertheless, it still makes an excellent foundation for fruit fillings.) Press into a pie dish and continue following the directions above.

## Peanut Butter Cookie Crust

¼ cup fructose
½ cup whole wheat flour
½ cup unbleached white flour
½ cup peanut butter
1 tsp. vanilla
1 tbsp. water
1 egg

In a small bowl mix together the fructose, whole wheat flour and white flour. Cut the peanut butter into this mixture using a pastry blender or 2 knives. Add the combined vanilla, water and egg and mix well to form a ball. Refrigerate for 1 hour. Roll out in circle large enough to fit a 9-inch pie shell. If pieces break off, they can easily be pressed together while being fitted into the pie shell. Press the edges down with a fork and prick the bottom and sides before baking. Bake at 425 degress for 10 minutes.

## Rice Flour and Sunflower Seed Pie Crust

½ cup rice flour
¾ cup ground sunflower seeds
1 tbsp. fructose
2 tbsps. bran
¼ cup melted margarine

Combine the first 4 ingredients and blend into the margarine. Press into a 9-inch pie dish even-ly. Bake 10 minutes at 400 degrees.

Pastries and Foundations

## Shredded Wheat and Peanut Crust

1 cup rolled shredded wheat
⅓ cup chopped salted peanuts
¼ cup fructose
3 tbsps. melted margarine or butter

To obtain the rolled shredded wheat I place about 1¼ cups spoon-sized shredded wheat in a paper sack and go over it firmly with a rolling pin. Combine this with the peanuts and fructose, mixing thoroughly. Pour the melted margarine into a baking dish 9 inches in diameter and 2 inches high. Add the first mixture to this and mix well. Press against the sides and bottom of the baking dish. Refrigerate for ½ hour before baking. For a baked shell place in 375 degree oven and bake for 15 to 20 minutes. For an unbaked shell follow the directions of the filling recipe.

## Vegetable Oil Pie Crust with Corn Meal

This crust is relatively low on fat, which has some health advantages. However, it does not freeze well.

¼ cup oil
¼ cup water
1 cup unbleached white flour
½ cup cornmeal
½ tsp. salt

Stir together the oil and water in a bowl. Sift together the flour, corn meal and salt and mix in thoroughly with the oil and water to make a ball. Flatten it and roll out between 2 sheets of waxed paper. Fit into pie tin. For a baked shell, bake for 10 to 15 minutes at 400 degrees. For an unbaked shell, follow the directions of the filling recipes. Makes enough for 1 crust pie. Double the recipe if you want a top crust.

## Whole Wheat Muerbe Teig

½ cup whole wheat flour
½ cup white flour
2 tbsps. fructose
4 tbsps. margarine or butter
1/8 tsp. salt
1 egg yolk
½ tsp. vanilla, or ¼ tsp. almond extract

Combine the flours, fructose and salt. Sift together. Cut in the shortening until coarsely blended. Stir together the egg yolk and flavoring. Add to the first mixture and mix thoroughly. You may either press this into the bottom and sides of a pie dish, or you may roll it out to fit the pie dish. It will roll more easily if you chill it in the refrigerator. For a baked pie crust, bake at 425 degrees until lightly browned, about 10 to 15 minutes.

## Party Cream Puffs

After much experimenting, I concluded that less shortening in proportion to flour than conventional recipes recommend gave me best results.

¾ cup flour
1 tsp. fructose
1 tsp. sesame seeds
1/8 tsp. salt
¾ cup water
¼ cup butter or margarine
3 eggs at room temperature

Combine flour, fructose, sesame seeds and salt. Bring the water and margarine to a boil in a sauce pan. Add the dry mixture and continue cooking, stirring constantly, until the mixture adheres to itself in a ball pulling away from the spoon. Let cool for three minutes. Beat in the eggs one at a time beating thoroughly after each addition. The batter is ready when a mound holds its shape in the spoon. Push well-rounded teaspoonfuls of the batter onto a greased baking sheet, forming the mounds, if necessary, so that they are higher in the center. Bake at 400 degrees for 10 minutes. Reduce heat to 350 degrees and bake for 20 minutes more, or until golden brown and firm. Turn off the oven and let cool in the oven for 15 minutes. Slit to let out any steam. These are good filled with fruits, creamy puddings, or any kind of pie filling. Also, they are excellent with creamed eggs, seafood, chicken, vegetables, and can be used as hors d'oeuvres. Fill just piror to serving so puffs do not become soggy.

# Apple Juice Crepes

1 cup unsweetened apple juice
2 tbsps. lemon juice
2 eggs
½ tsp. salt
2 tbsps. fructose
½ cup whole wheat flour

Beat together the apple juice, lemon juice and eggs until well-blended. Stir the fructose and salt into the whole wheat flour and beat into the first mixture. Pour about 2 tbsps. of this mixture into a buttered, heated 6-inch skillet turning the pan to cover evenly. Cook on one side only until the visible side is no longer shiny. Turn onto a wooden board, cooked side up. Spread with jam or marmalade and roll up, folding over the ends to make an envelope. This is also good filled with about 1 tbsp. of sliced fruit.

I have also found the Apple-Cheese Filling (see recipe) very successful. Follow the filling recipe up to the point of baking, and use 1 tbsp. for each crepe. Crepes can be made ahead of time and placed in the refrigerator. When ready to serve, fry until lightly browned on both sides. These can be served with your favorite syrups, sour cream, whipped cream or yogurt. If you want to keep the envelopes for more than 12 hours, they should be frozen. Makes about 16 crepes.

## Fructose French Meringue

To make successful meringues it is important to choose a day that is not humid. The egg whites should be at room temperature at least; better still, a little warmer. I let them rest in my oven which has a pilot light so that the oven is warmer than the kitchen; or you may set the bowl containing egg whites in a pan of hot water, but not hot enough or long enough to congeal them. I have experimented with many different ways of preparing pans for baking meringues and have had success brushing the pan with equal parts of salad oil and liquid lecithin.

1 cup fructose
6 tbsps. water
3 egg whites
¼ tsp. cream of tartar
1 tsp. rum or vanilla (optional)

Place the fructose in a heavy kettle at low heat until it is melted and golden. Slowly add the water and let cook until just past the soft-ball stage, about 240 degrees on a candy thermometer. Meanwhile, add the cream of tartar to the egg whites in a large bowl and beat until the egg whites hold soft peaks. **Very** slowly add the syrup beating constantly. Beat in the flavoring. This can be spread in a 9-inch spring form or pie tin, greased with the lecithin oil combination mentioned above, to make a foundation for fruit filling, custards, ice cream, etc. Or you can place 2 tbsps. at a time on a prepared cookie sheet to make individual meringues. Place in a cold oven and set the temperature at 250 degrees. Bake until golden, about 1 hour. Leave in oven until cool. Makes about 2 dozen little meringues or 1 nine-inch foundation.

## Fructose French Meringue Topping

Follow the recipe for Fructose French Meringue foundation (page 78) and spread on top of pie. Bake as directed.

## Rolled Strudel Dough

2 cups flour
1 tbsp. fructose
¼ tsp. salt
1 egg
3 tbsps. vegetable oil
⅔ cup approximately ice water
1 tbsp. melted margarine or butter

Mix the flour, fructose and salt in a bowl. In another small bowl or cup beat the egg, oil and about ¼ cup of the ice water together. Using the bottom of a cup, make a well in the flour mixture. Pour the egg mixture into this well and work the dry ingredients into this. Slowly add enough ice water to make a kneadable dough, mixing thoroughly. Knead for about 5 minutes to make a smooth dough. For making a strudel cut the dough in half and roll each half in an oblong about 9 inches by 15 inches. Brush the tops with melted margarine or butter and cover with chosen filling. Roll up lengthwise, seal the edges, place in a greased cookie tin (it may be necessary to lay it on the diagonal or to curve the roll slightly), brush the roll with melted margarine or butter and bake at 375 degrees for about 50 minutes. About half way through the baking, brush the tops with more melted margarine or butter. After removing from oven, slice with a very sharp knife with a slow, sawing motion. Makes about 1 dozen slices.

# Apple Strudel

4 cups thinly sliced apples
½ cup chopped raisins
½ cup fructose
1 tsp. cinnamon
¼ tsp. nutmeg
1 cup bread crumbs
1 tbsp. margarine or butter
½ cup sliced almonds
6 sheets of prepared filo pastry or 1 Rolled
Strudel Dough (see recipe)
2 tbsps. melted margarine or butter

Mix together in a bowl the apples, raisins, fructose and spices. Prepare 3 sheets of the filo dough in the following manner: Lay a sheet of filo dough on a board and brush ½ of it with melted shortening. Fold to cover this with the other half and brush again with melted shortening. Repeat the process with 2 more sheets and place them evenly on top the first sheet so that you have 6 layers of greased half sheets of filo dough, roughly 14 inches by 7 inches. Sprinkle ½ cup of the bread crumbs over this. Place ½ the apple mixture evenly over the bread crumbs and sprinkle ¼ cup of the sliced almonds over the apple mixture. Roll up jelly-roll fashion lengthwise so that you have a roll approximately 14 inches long. Moisten the edge and press together. Grease the top and place on a buttered cookie tin. Repeat this entire process using the remaining 3 sheets of filo dough. Apple strudel can also be made using Rolled Strudel Dough, cutting it in half and rolling out to an oblong 15 inches by 9 inches. Bake at 350 degrees for 50 to 60 minutes. Cut into 1½-inch slices.

## Bean Curd and Pineapple Strudel

This recipe is another delicious way of adapting the Orient's healthful contribution, tofu, into our melting pot cuisine.

¾ cup drained tofu
¼ cup fructose
2 egg yolks
1/8 tsp. salt
¾ cup drained crushed pineapple
⅓ cup chopped dates
½ cup bread crumbs, toasted in 1 tbsp. margarine or butter
½ recipe Rolled Strudel Dough (see recipe)
1 tbsp. melted margarine or butter

Pat the tofu dry with a paper towel. Place in the top of a double boiler with the fructose, egg yolks, crushed pineapple salt and dates. Stir over boiling water, mashing the tofu, until thick and spreadable. Roll the strudel dough to a thin oblong, approximately 9 inches by 15 inches. Spread melted butter over the dough. Sprinkle the toasted bread crumbs over this evenly. Lay the tofu mixture on top of the crumbs in heaping tablespoons and spread lightly with a spatula. Roll up lengthwise, jelly-roll fashion, to make a roll about 15 inches long. Place seam-side down on a greased cookie tin. Brush the top with melted butter or margarine. Bake at 375 degrees about 50 to 60 minutes. Brush the top with melted butter again about half way through the baking time. Slice with a very sharp knife and a sawing motion. Makes about 1 dozen slices.

## Baklava

¼ lb. chopped almonds (about 1 cup)
2 tbsps. fructose
2 tbsps. fine dried bread crumbs
¼ tsp. cinnamon
1/8 tsp. nutmeg
7 sheets prepared filo pastry
3 tbsps. melted butter
18 whole cloves
1 recipe Lemon Syrup (see recipe)

In a small bowl combine thoroughly the first 5 ingredients and set aside. Butter a 6-inch by 10-inch baking dish. Take 1 sheet of the filo pastry and dab melted butter on half of it (I use a pointillist technique on this rather than a brush stroke), using about 1 teaspoon of melted butter per sheet. Fold the unbuttered half on top of this to form a double layer and butter the second surface. Lay this in the baking dish. There will be some overlap. Repeat with another sheet of filo so that you will have 4 layers in all from 2 sheets. Sprinkle ⅓ of the filling mixture over this. Fold the excess filo over the edges. (Some recipes suggest trimming it instead.) Prepare another sheet of filo with melted butter as before and place over the filling. Sprinkle this with another third of the filling and fold edges as before. Add another sheet of prepared filo and top with the remaining filo. (Since these are doubled they will make 4 layers.) Fold these last edges under. Cut into 18 pieces, 6 slices the long way and 3 the short. Place a clove into the top of each piece. Bake for 1 hour until golden brown. Pour hot Lemon Syrup (see recipe) over the top. Let cool before serving. This adaptation is less rich than the traditional Greek recipe.

## Baklava
## adapted to fructose syrup

¼ lb. chopped almonds
2 tbsps. fine dried bread crumbs
¼ tsp. cinnamon
1/8 tsp. nutmeg
7 sheets prepared filo pastry
3 tbsps. melted butter
1½ tbsps. 90% fructose syrup
18 whole cloves
1 recipe lemon syrup

Mix together the almonds, bread crumbs, cin-namon and nutmeg. Stir together the melted but-ter and fructose syrup. Follow the directions for making Baklava, the only exception being that you substitute the combination of melted butter and fructose syrup wherever melted butter is call-ed for in the recipe.

## Yugoslavian Pinwheels

¼ cup chopped raisins
¼ cup chopped nuts
2 tbsps. toasted fine bread crumbs
1 tbsp. fructose
½ tsp. cinnamon
1 tbsp. lemon juice
1 tsp. grated lemon rind
4 sheets filo pastry
2 tbsps. butter, melted
14 whole cloves
½ cup lemon syrup

Mix together thoroughly the first 7 ingredients. Dab ½ of a sheet of filo with melted butter. Fold to cover this with the other half and dab butter on top of it. Lay this prepared sheet on top of a piece of waxed paper. Repeat this process with a second sheet of filo so that you have 4 layers. Sprinkle this evenly with ⅓ the raisin-nut mixture. Repeat this process with a second sheet of filo so that you have 4 layers. Sprinkle this evenly with ⅓ the raisin-nut mixture. Repeat the double buttering of ⅓ sheet of filo already used and cover the sprinkled raisin-nut mixture with it. Sprinkle another ⅓ of the raisin-nut mixture on top of this. Again cover with a doubled layer of buttered filo and sprinkle with the remaining ⅓ of raisin-nut mixture. Form the layers into a tight roll, jelly-roll fashion, lengthwise. Brush the last edge with water, lightly, to help it adhere. Press the 14 cloves into the roll evenly spaced about 1 inch apart and slice the roll with a sharp knife between the cloves to form 14 pinwheels. Place these, cut side up, close together on a greased baking dish. Brush melted butter on the tops. Bake at 350 degrees about ½ hour until golden. Pour the syrup evenly over the pinwheels and let stand a few hours before serving. Makes 14 pinwheels.

# Pie Fillings

## Apple Yogurt Plum Jam Pie

1 quart sliced apples
2 tbsps. margarine
½ cup fructose
1 tbsp. cornstarch
1 tsp. cinnamon
1 cup plain yogurt
2 tbsps. plum jam
3 egg yolks

Over very low heat melt the margarine in a sauce pan. Toss in the sliced apples and continue cooking. Combine ¼ cup of the fructose with the cornstarch and cinnamon. Stir this into the apple-margarine mixture and cook until the apples are slightly tender, about 10 minutes, stirring occasionally to prevent scorching. Blend the egg yolks with the remaining ¼ cup fructose. Mix thoroughly with yogurt and plum jam. Pour the cooked apple mixture into the pie crust of your choice. Top with the combined egg yolk, fructose, yogurt and plum jam. I like this with the Rice Flour and Sunflower Seed Pie Crust (see recipe). Bake at 375 degrees about 45 minutes until custard sets.

## Kiss-With-Squeeze Apple Pie

One of the earliest jingles I remember:
Apple pie without the cheese
Is like a kiss without the squeeze.
This pie should help you get plenty of both.

7 cups apple slices
1 tbsp. margarine or butter
½ to ⅔ cup fructose, depending on sweetness of
   apples
2 tbsps. flour
1/8 tsp. salt
1/8 tsp. nutmeg
1 tsp. cinnamon
1 recipe Cheese Pastry
1 recipe Cheese and Whole
   Wheat Streusel Topping

Heat the margarine or butter and apple slices in a sauce pan until apples are tender but firm. Combine the fructose, flour, salt, nutmeg and cinnamon and stir lightly through the apples. Bake the cheese pastry alone at 425 degrees for 10 minutes. Turn the apple mixture into the pastry and sprinkle streusel evenly over whole pie. Return to the 425-degree oven and bake until streusel is golden brown, about 25 to 30 minutes.

## Lemon Meringue Pie

¾ cup fructose
1/8 tsp. salt
6 tbsps. cornstarch
2 cups boiling water
⅓ cup lemon juice
¼ to ⅓ cup finely grated lemon rind
3 eggs separated
1 baked 9-inch pie shell
Meringue Topping (see recipe)

In top of double boiler combine the fructose, salt and cornstarch. Slowly stir in the boiling water. Cook over hot water, stirring until thick. Beat the egg yolks in a cup. Gradually, add about ½ cup of the cooked mixture to egg yolks, stirring constantly. Pour this back into the cooked mixture and cook over hot water for 3 minutes, stirring constantly. Remove from heat and add the lemon juice and lemon rind. Let cool, stirring occasionally, before putting into pie shell. Spread the meringue on top of the pie lightly but making sure that it covers the custard completely to the edge of the pie. Bake at 325 degrees until lightly browned, 15 to 20 minutes.

## Yogurt Banana Pie

2 tbsps. margarine
¼ cup ground sunflower seeds
2 tbsps. fructose
2 tbsps. bran
2 tbsps. wheat germ
½ tsp. cinnamon
1 cup sliced banana
1 cup plain yogurt
2 eggs, separated
2 tbsps. lemon juice
2 tbsps. grated lemon rind
¼ cup fructose

Melt margarine in bottom of 9-inch pie dish. Combine the ground sunflower seeds, 2 tbsps. fructose, cinnamon, bran and wheat germ. Sprinkle evenly into the margarine and press lightly with back of spoon. Cover evenly with sliced bananas. Mix thoroughly the yogurt, egg yolks, lemon juice and rind and fructose. Beat egg whites until stiff and fold into this mixture. Spoon the mixture evenly over the bananas and crust in the pie dish. Bake at 325 degrees 40 to 50 minutes until a toothpick comes out clean.

Pie Fillings

## Pumpkin Apple-Butter Pie

If you don't want to oppose tradition, but are tired of the same old pumpkin pie every Thanksgiving, try this one.

1 cup pumpkin, cooked or canned
1 cup Apple Butter (see recipe)
1 cup evaporated milk
2 eggs
½ cup fructose
2 tbsps. unbleached white flour
1 tsp. cinnamon
¼ tsp. ginger
¼ tsp. nutmeg
¼ tsp. ground cloves

Beat together in a bowl the pumpkin, apple butter, evaporated milk and eggs. Sift together the remaining ingredients and add to the mixture in the bowl. Beat until well-blended. Turn into an unbaked piecrust and bake at 425 degrees for 15 minutes. Reduce heat to 350 degrees and continue baking until knife inserted in pie comes out clean, about 50 to 60 minutes. This works very well with the Vegetable Oil Pie Crust with Corn Meal (see recipe).

## Prune Whip Pie with Chestnuts

3 eggs, separated
3 tbsps. fructose
½ cup coarsely chopped chestnuts
⅔ cup sliced prunes, unsweetened moist pack
3 tbsps. lemon juice

Beat the egg yolks with the fructose until light. Beat in the chestnuts, prunes and lemon juice. Beat the egg whites until they hold soft peaks. Fold into the first mixture. Turn into an unbaked pie shell, I like the Almond-Coconut Crust (see recipe) for this. Bake at 350 degrees until lightly browned, 20 to 30 minutes. Makes one 9-inch pie.

## Coffee-Flavored Chiffon Pie

1 cup boiling water
2 tsps. instant coffee
¼ cup cold water
1 envelope (1 tbsp.) gelatin
3 egg separated
⅓ cup fructose
1/8 tsp. salt
¼ cup fructose
1/8 tsp. cream of tartar

Dissolve the instant coffee in the boiling water and let stand to cool. Soften the gelatin in the ¼ cup cold water. In the top of a double boiler beat together the egg yolks, ⅓ cup fructose and salt. Slowly stir in the lukewarm coffee. Heat over hot water until the mixture coats the spoon, about 8 minutes. Stir in the softened gelatin and cook until the gelatin dissolves. Place in the refrigerator until the mixture becomes syrupy thick. Mix together ¼ cup fructose and cream of tartar. Beat the egg whites until they hold soft peaks. Slowly beat in the fructose mixture. Fold the gelatin mixture gently into the egg whites. Pour into a baked 9-inch pie shell and chill until firm. If you wish, you can top this with whipped cream, or sprinkle ¼ cup chopped almonds over the top. Makes one 9-inch pie.

## Banana Date-Nut Fiesta Pie

1 Coffee-Flavored Chiffon Pie Filling (see recipe)
¼ cup chopped dates
¼ cup chopped nuts
1 cup thin banana slices
1 recipe Whole Wheat Muerbe Teig baked pie
   crust
1 cup whipping cream

Fold the nuts and dates into the finished pie filling. Spread ⅓ of filling onto the bottom of the baked Merbe Teig crust. Place ½ the banana slices evenly over this and cover with another ⅓ of the filling. Top this with the remaining banana slices and cover them with the remainder of the filling. Refrigerate at least 3 hours. A few minutes before serving, whip the cream and swirl over the pie. If you wish, garnish with a handful of chopped nuts.

Pie Fillings

**89**

## Lemon Chiffon Pie

1 envelope gelatin
¾ cup fructose
1/8 tsp. salt
3 eggs, separated
⅓ cup lemon juice
½ cup water
2 tsps. grated lemon rind
2 tbsps. margarine or butter

In the top of a double boiler mix together the gelatin, 6 tbsps. of the fructose and the salt. Beat together the egg yolks, lemon juice and water and stir into the gelatin mixture. Cook over hot water stirring constantly until gelatin is dissolved. Add margarine or butter and lemon rind and continue cooking and stirring until the margarine or butter is melted. Chill until the mixture is thick but not solid. Beat the egg whites until stiff. Slowly add the remaining fructose while beating continuously. Fold the gelatin mixture into the beaten egg white mixture. Pour into a baked pie crust and chill until firm. You may wish to top this with whipped cream or serve a bowl of whipped cream separately. Makes one 9-inch pie.

## Lemon Chiffon Pie
## adapted to fructose syrup

½ cup water
1 envelope (1 tbsp.) gelatin
½ cup 90% fructose syrup
1/8 tsp. salt
3 eggs, separated
2 tbsps. margarine or butter
⅓ cup lemon juice
2 tsps. grated lemon rind

Combine the cold water and gelatin in the top of a double boiler. Stir in the fructose syrup and salt. Beat the egg yolks together with the lemon juice and stir into the sauce pan mixture. Cook over hot water, stirring constantly, until the mixture coats the spoon. Add the margarine or butter and continue cooking and stirring until the margarine or butter is melted. Chill until the mixture is thick but not solid. In a bowl large enough to hold the entire ingredients beat the egg whites until stiff. Gently fold the sauce pan mixture and the lemon rind into the beaten egg whites. Pour into a baked pie crust and chill until firm.

## Orange Chiffon Pie

Use ½ cup orange juice and 1 tbsp. lemon juice instead of the ⅓ cup lemon juice in the above recipe. Substitute 2 tsps. grated orange rind for the 2 tsps. grated lemon rind. With these two exceptions, follow the Lemon Chiffon Pie recipe.

## Mock Chestnut Chiffon Pie

This recipe has its roots in a conversation that I had with a woman on a train in France who told me how Frenchwomen substituted lima beans for chestnuts during the war. My first thought was that it was too unusual to include in this book, but my tasting friends felt that it was another example of excellence in flavor and nutritional value.

1 envelope gelatin
¼ cup cold water
2 eggs, separated
¾ cup fructose
½ cup yogurt
1/8 tsp. salt
1 tsp. cinnamon
¼ tsp. nutmeg
¼ tsp. ground cloves
1 tsp. vanilla
¼ tsp. cream of tartar
1 cup cooked baby lima beans
½ cup raisins or dates
½ cup whipping cream
    (optional)

Combine the gelatin with cold water. Beat the egg yolks and ½ cup of the fructose in a sauce pan. Stir in the yogurt, salt and spices. Cook over medium heat stirring constantly just until it begins to boil. Add the softened gelatin. Puree the lima beans in a blender or by forcing through a sieve. Add the pureed lima beans to the sauce pan mixture. Heat again, stirring constantly, until the gelatin is dissolved. Let cool. Add the cream of tartar to the egg whites. Beat until they hold soft peaks. Slowly beat in remaining fructose. Stir the raisins and vanilla into the sauce pan mixture. Fold the sauce pan mixture into the beaten egg whites. Whip the cream, if used, and fold into chiffon mixture. Turn into a 9-inch pie crust and refrigerate until firm.

Pie Fillings

**91**

# Refrigerator Desserts

## California Gold Cheese Dessert

1½ cups dry curd cottage cheese
2 eggs separated
½ cup milk
⅓ cup fructose
¼ tsp. salt
2 tbsps. lemon juice
2 tbsps. grated orange rind
1½ cups persimmon pulp (or other fruit in
  season)
¼ cup fructose
2 tbsps. lemon juice
¼ cup orange juice
¼ cup water
2 envelopes unsweetened
  gelatin
2 tbsps. fructose

Place in a blender the cottage cheese, egg yolks, milk, ⅓ cup fructose, salt, 2 tbsps. lemon juice and grated orange rind. Blend a few seconds, just long enough to be thoroughly mixed. Place the persimmon pulp, ¼ cup fructose and 2 tbsps. lemon juice in a sauce pan and bring to a boil. Remove from heat. In the top of a double boiler combine the gelatin, 2 tbsps. fructose, ¼ cup water and ¼ cup orange juice. Heat just until the gelatin is dissolved. Divide this into 2 equal portions, approximately ¼ cup each, and stir 1 portion into the blender mixture and the other into the persimmon mixture. Beat the egg whites until fluffy. Fold ½ the egg whites into the blender mixture, the other into the persimmon mixture. Pour the persimmon mixture into a 1 quart mold and chill for 1 hour. Remove from refrigerator and pour over the persimmon mixture the cheese-blender mixture. Refrigerate until firm. Unmold when ready to serve. This makes a pretty dessert if you start the mold with ½ the persimmon; when firm, add ½ the cheese; then later, the remaining persimmon; and again when firm, the remaining cheese.

## Carob-Mocha Bavarian Cream

⅓ cup fructose
1/8 tsp. salt
1 tbsp. powdered coffee
1 envelope (1 tbsp.) gelatin
2 eggs, separated
¾ cup milk
1 tsp. vanilla
1/8 tsp. cream of tartar
½ cup whipping cream, or (½ cup ice water, ½
   skimmed milk powder, 1 tbsp. lemon juice)
½ cup carob powder

Mix together in top of double boiler 2 tbsps. of the fructose, salt, powdered coffee and gelatin. Beat together the egg yolks and milk, and stir into the mixture. Cook over hot water until the gelatin has dissolved. Remove from heat and stir in the carob powder and vanilla until well-blended. Chill, stirring occasionally, until thick but not firm. In a bowl large enough to hold a quart comfortably beat the egg whites until they hold peaks. Add the cream of tartar and gradually beat in the remaining fructose. Fold in the gelatin mixture. Whip the cream and fold into the mixture in the bowl. Chill until firm. If you use the skim milk powder, combine with the ice water, whip and add lemon juice. Fold into the mixture in the bowl.

## Carob-Mocha Pie

The above recipe makes an excellent pie filling. I like to put it into a Peanut Butter Pie Crust (see recipe) and sprinkle it with chopped peanuts.

## Pineapple Biscuit Tortoni

4 egg yolks
½ cup fructose
1 cup juice from unsweetened crushed pineapple
1 cup coarse cookie crumbs
½ cup chopped nuts
½ cup crushed pineapple
1 cup whipping cream

Stir together the egg yolks, fructose and pineapple juice in the top of a double boiler. Cook over hot water, stirring constantly, until the mixture coats the spoon. Remove from heat and stir in the cookie crumbs, chopped nuts and crushed pineapple. Let cool while whipping the cream to form soft mounds. Fold the first mixture into the whipped cream, mixing gently. Turn into a mold or refrigerator trays. Cover and place in freezer. Makes 8 to 10 servings.

## Date and Grape-Nut Mousse

1 tbsp. gelatin
¼ cup cold water
¼ cup boiling hot water
¾ cup chopped dates
½ fructose
½ cup water
1 tbsp. lemon juice
½ cup Grape-Nuts, or chopped nuts of your
    choice
1 cup whipping cream

Soften the gelatin in ¼ cup cold water. Add the ¼ cup boiling hot water and stir until the gelatin is dissolved. Bring the dates, fructose and ½ cup water to a boil and let simmer for 3 minutes. Add the gelatin mixture and stir thoroughly. Let cool. Stir in the lemon juice and Grape-Nuts or other nuts. Whip the cream until it forms soft mounds. Fold together with the first mixture. Turn into a 1-quart mold and freeze. Like any of the whipped cream desserts, this can also be used as a pie filling. Serves 6 to 8.

Refrigerator Desserts

## Frosty Grape-Orange Yogurt Pudding

3 tbsps. cornstarch
½ cup fructose
1 envelope (1 tbsp.) gelatin
¼ cup water
2 cups grapes, removed from stems
1 egg
2 cups orange sections cut into chunks
1 cup plain yogurt
¼ tsp. nutmeg
¼ tsp. ground cloves
¼ tsp. cinnamon

In a saucepan combine the cornstarch, fructose and gelatin. Stir in the water. If the grapes have seeds, remove them. Do not cut seedless grapes. I like to combine a variety of grapes for color. Add the grapes to the mixture in the saucepan and cook over low heat, stirring until thick. Beat the egg. Then combine it with a small amount of the saucepan mixture, adding slowly a half cup in all. Pour this back into the saucepan and cook for 5 minutes over low heat. Do not allow this to boil. Stir the spices and oranges into the yogurt and fold it into the mixture in the saucepan. Pour into freezer trays, cover and freeze. For a smoother dessert, stir thoroughly when frozen to the slushy stage. Makes about 5 cups, enough to serve 8 to 10 people.

**Frosty Grape-Orange Yogurt Pudding**
**adapted to fructose syrup**

1 envelope (1 tbsp.) gelatin
¼ cup water
⅓ cup 90% fructose syrup
3 tbsps. cornstarch
2 cups grapes, removed from stems
1 egg
2 cups orange sections cut into chunks
1 cup plain yogurt
¼ tsp. nutmeg
¼ tsp. ground cloves
¼ tsp. cinnamon

In a sauce pan combine the gelatin and cold water. Stir in the fructose syrup and cornstarch. Add the grapes and cook over low heat, stirring, until thick. As described in the above recipe, add the beaten egg and continue following the directions.

**Flavored Yogurts**

As you know, many attractive, flavored yogurts are available. They tend to be high in sugar which research indicates is less good for you than fructose. But flavor does add to the enjoyment of yogurt. You can create your own flavors easily with fructose. Here are a few suggestions.

**Carob Mocha Yogurt**

1 cup prepared plain yogurt
4 tsps. carob powder
1 tsp. instant coffee powder
2 to 3 tbsps. fructose, as you prefer

Mix these ingredients together thoroughly — and enjoy!

## Carob Mocha Yogurt
### adapted to fructose syrup

1 cup plain yogurt
1½ tbsps. 90% fructose syrup, more or less to
    taste
4 tsps. carob powder
1 tsp. instant coffee

Mix these ingredients together thoroughly.

## Fructose Syrup Yogurt

Add 2 to 3 tbsps. of any of the syrup recipes in this book to 1 cup of plain prepared yogurt.

## Yogurt with Preserves

Add 2 to 3 tbsps. of any of the marmalades, jams or jellies recipes in this book to 1 cup of yogurt.

These flavored yogurts are excellent to use as sauces with custards, puddings or spooned over fresh fruit. They also make tasty snacks by themselves.

## Fresh Fruit Yogurt

½ cup diced fresh fruit
1 to 2 tsps. fructose, depending on tartness of
    fruit
1 tbsp. lemon juice or other fruit juice
1 cup plain yogurt
1 tbsp. sliced almonds (optional)

In a small bowl stir the fructose into the juice. Add the diced fruit and toss to coat it evenly. Let stand at least 10 minutes to bring out flavor. Stir in the yogurt and top with the almonds, if used. A sprinkling of other chopped nuts or toasted sesame seeds may also be used.


## Frozen Apricot Cream

1 cup chopped dried apricots
⅓ cup fructose
1 cup water
1 tbsp. (envelope) gelatin
¼ cup cold water
2 tbsps. lemon juice
1 tsp. grated lemon rind
1 cup whipping cream

In a sauce pan simmer the apricots, fructose and water for about 10 minutes to make a thin syrup. Soften the gelatin in ¼ cup cold water. Add to the sauce pan and stir until the gelatin dissolves. Stir in the lemon juice and rind. Let cool to room temperature. Beat the whipped cream until it holds mounds, being careful not to let it get buttery. Fold the sauce pan mixture into the whipped cream. Turn into a 6-cup mold. Cover with foil and freeze. Makes 10 to 12 servings. This can also be turned into a cookie crumb crust, sprinkled with cookie crumbs and served as a kind of ice cream pie.

Refrigerator Desserts

**99**

## Frozen Cranberry-Tofu Cream

At one time tofu could be found only in Orien-tal markets. Now, since many are aware of its ad-vantages, high protein and calcium at a relatively low cost, it's available in many supermarkets. This recipe overcomes the blandness that some find objectionable in tofu.

1 cup cranberries
1 ¼ cups fructose
2 cups drained tofu
1 envelope gelatin
¼ cup cold water
2 eggs, separated
1 cup yogurt
1 cup oranges cut in chunks
1 tbsp. orange rind

Wash and pick over the cranberries. Heat in a sauce pan with ½ cup of the fructose over low heat, stirring, until the cranberries have popped. Cut the tofu into chunks and whisk it with the cranberry mixture in your blender. Soften the gelatin in the cold water. Place the egg yolks, yogurt and 6 tbsps. of the fructose in the top of a double boiler. Cook over hot water, stirring, until mixture coats the spoon, about 5 minutes. Add the softened gelatin and continue cooking over hot water until the gelatin dissolves. Remove from heat and mix thoroughly with the tofu cranberry mixture. Chill until mixture forms mounds when dropped from a spoon. Beat the egg whites until stiff but not dry and add the re-maining fructose gradually as you continue beating. Fold the chilled mixture, oranges and rind into the beaten egg white mixture. Pour into molds or freezer trays, cover and place in freezer compartment of refrigerator. Makes about 6 cups.

## Frozen Fruit-Nut Custard

1 tbsp. cornstarch
⅓ cup fructose
pinch of salt
2 eggs, separated
½ cup milk
½ cup pineapple juice
1 cup diced fruit of your choice
1 tsp. vanilla, or ½ tsp. almond extract
½ cup whipping cream (or ½ cup skimmed milk
    powder, ½ cup ice water and 1 tbsp. lemon
    juice)
¼ cup chopped almonds or other nuts

Combine the first 3 ingredients in the top of a double boiler. Add the milk and pineapple juice and cook over hot water stirring constantly until syrupy. Beat egg yolks. Pour into them slowly about ¼ cup of the heated mixture. Pour the egg yolk mixture back into the top of the double boiler and cook over hot water, stirring constantly, until thick. Add the fruit and nuts and let cool. Beat the egg whites until firm but not stiff and fold the custard into them. Whip the cream, or if you are using the skimmed milk, add it to the ice water and whip. Then add the lemon juice. Add the vanilla or almond extract. (I use almond extract when using almonds. I also prefer the whipped skim milk powder.) Fold this into the combined custard-egg white mixture. Turn into two refrigerator trays. Cover with aluminum foil and freeze. Stir these when slushy and return to freezer. Makes 5 cups.

## Layered Refrigerator Cake

12 Little Brown Babas (see recipe)
12 tbsps. Rum Syrup (see recipe) or other syrup
1 recipe Biscuit Tortoni

One hour before separation, prick the babas with a fork and sprinkle each with 1 tbsp. syrup. Refrigerate for easier slicing. Slice 10 of the babas horizontally into thin circles. Chop the remaining two into coarse crumbs. Line a 9-inch cake dish with half of the slices. Spoon ½ the Biscuit Tortoni evenly over the slices. Add another layer of slices and cover them with the remaining ½ of the Biscuit Tortoni. Distribute the crumbs evenly over the top. Place in freezer. Makes about 8 servings. For variety any of the whipped cream desserts or pie fillings may be used instead of the Biscuit Tortoni.

## Mandarin Cream Pie Filling

One of my favorites. This recipe is not only delicious and nutritious, but very useful if you must avoid eggs and milk.

2 cups peeled mandarin segments (tangerines or tangelos)
¼ cup fructose plus ⅓ cup fructose
1 tbsp. gelatin
¼ cup cold water
¼ cup boiling hot water
1½ cups drained and dried tofu
¼ tsp. salt
1 tsp. vanilla
2 tbsps. grated mandarin rind
2 tbsps. grated coconut, optional

Cut the mandarin segments in thirds crosswise, removing the seeds. Place 1 cup of the segments in a small bowl and stir in ¼ cup fructose. In a large bowl soften the gelatin in the cold water. Stir in the hot water until the gelatin is completely dissolved. Combine the remaining cup of mandarin chunks with the tofu, which has been drained and patted dry with paper towels, salt and vanilla. Run this through the blender until smooth, one half at a time. Mix thoroughly with the softened gelatin and 1 tbsp. of the grated rind. Stir in the first cup of mandarin segments and fructose. Pour into a mold or baked crust. Sprinkle the top with the remaining grated rind and, if you wish, the coconut. Refrigerate until firm. Makes 6 to 8 servings. This recipe adapts very well to berries or other fruits.

Refrigerator Desserts

### Mandarin Cream Pie Filling
### adapted to fructose syrup

2 cups mandarin peeled segments (tangerines or tangelos)
½ cup 90% fructose syrup
1 tbsp. (1 envelope) gelatin
¼ cup cold water
¼ cup boiling hot water
1½ cups drained and dried tofu
¼ tsp. salt
1 tsp. vanilla
2 tbsps. grated mandarin rind
2 tbsps. grated coconut, optional

Cut the mandarin segments in thirds crosswise, removing the seeds. Place 1 cup of the segments in a small bowl and stir in ¼ cup fructose syrup. In a large bowl combine the gelatin and the cold water. Stir in the hot water until the gelatin is completely dissolved. Combine the tofu, which has been drained and patted dry with paper towels, with the remaining cup of mandarin chunks, salt and vanilla. Run this, one-half at a time, through a blender just until smooth. Pour the blender mixture into the softened gelatin and stir. Add 1 tbsp. of the grated rind, the remaining ¼ cup of fructose syrup and the first cup of sweetened mandarin segments. Stir thoroughly and pour into a baked crust, if you desire a pie, or a mold or a bowl. Sprinkle the top with the remaining grated rind and, if you wish, the coconut. Refrigerate until firm. Makes 6-8 servings.

## Pineapple and Chestnut Ice Cream

1 cup pineapple juice, unsweetened
1 tbsp. gelatin (1 envelope)
1 cup crushed pineapple, unsweetened
1 cup diced chestnuts
1 cup fructose
2 eggs, separated
2 tbsps. lemon juice
1 cup whipping cream

Soften the gelatin in ¼ cup of the pineapple juice. In a sauce pan bring to a boil ½ cup of the fructose, the remaining pineapple juice, the crushed pineapple and the diced chestnuts from chestnuts which have been peeled and skinned. (See recipe for Taffy Chestnuts.) Add gelatin mixture and stir over hot water until the gelatin is dissolved. In a small bowl beat the egg yolks. Pour, 1 tablespoon at a time, ¼ cup of the sauce pan mixture into the egg yolks, stirring thoroughly after each addition. Pour the egg yolk mixture back into the sauce pan and, stirring constantly, cook over hot water for about 10 minutes. Remove from heat and add the lemon juice, mixing thoroughly. Cover the sauce pan and place in refrigerator until the mixture is the consistency of uncooked egg whites. Beat the egg whites until firm but not stiff. Add the remaining ½ cup fructose slowly as you continue beating. Fold into the sauce pan mixture. In a chilled bowl, beat the cold whipping cream until thick but not buttery. Fold into the sauce pan mixture. Pour into a mold or refrigerator trays. Cover and freeze. This makes about 6 cups, or about 12 servings, although at my house 6 people will make it disappear.

# Creamy Lemon Whip

3 eggs, separated
6 tbsps. lemon juice
⅔ cup fructose
1 tsp. grated lemon rind
1 tbsp. (1 envelope) gelatin
¼ cup cold water
½ cup hot water
1 cup whipping cream

Beat the egg yolks, lemon juice and ⅓ cup of the fructose together in the top of a double boiler. Cook over hot water until mixture coats the spoon, stirring constantly. Soften the gelatin in the cold water. Add the boiling hot water and stir until the gelatin is dissolved. Combine the two mixtures, stirring well, and allow to cool until syrupy thick. Meanwhile beat the egg whites until they form soft peaks and continue beating, adding the remainder of the fructose. When the gelatin mixture is syrupy, beat it to a froth. Add the grated lemon rind and fold together with the egg white mixture. Whip the cream until it holds soft mounds, being careful not to overbeat. Fold this into the combined gelatin and egg white mixtures, mixing gently without beating. Turn into a mold or refrigerator trays. Cover and freeze. Makes about 8 to 10 servings. This can also be used as an ice cream pie filling.

## Pineapple-Plum Yogurt Dessert

1 cup canned crushed pineapple
⅔ cup plum jam
2 tbsps. (2 envelopes) unflavored gelatin
2 tbsps. lemon juice
½ cup fructose
¼ tsp. salt
3 eggs, separated
2 cups yogurt
¼ tsp. cream of tartar

In top of a double boiler, stir together the jam and pineapple. Sprinkle the gelatin over this and cook over hot water stirring constantly until the gelatin is dissolved. Stir in the lemon juice and 2 tbsps. of fructose. Beat together the egg yolks and the yogurt. Stir into the fruit and gelatin mixture. Cook over hot water for 5 minutes stirring constantly. Mix the cream of tartar and the salt into the remaining fructose. Beat the egg whites until they hold a peak. Adding slowly, beat in the fructose. Fold the fruit and gelatin mixture into the egg whites. Pour into 8 serving glasses or bowls and chill until firm. Makes 8 servings.

## Ricotta Ribbon Mold

1 envelope gelatin
¼ cup cold water
¼ cup boiling hot water
2 cups ricotta cheese
½ cup fructose
2 tbsps. lemon juice
1 tbsp. grated lemon rind
½ cup drained crushed
   pineapple
½ cup cranberry sauce
   (see recipe)

Soften the gelatin in the cold water. Add the boiling water and stir until gelatin dissolves. Beat together the fructose, ricotta cheese, lemon juice and rind. Combine with the dissolved gelatin and beat with an electric mixer or vigorously by hand until smooth. Mix ⅓ of this mixture, about ⅔ of a cup, with the crushed pineapple and spread in the bottom of a mold. Mix another ⅓ with the cranberry sauce. Spoon evenly over the pineapple mixture in the mold. Use a light touch so as not to disturb the bottom layer. Top with the remaining ricotta and gelatin mixture, again spooning lightly. Refrigerate until firm. Makes 8 to 10 servings.

## Cranberry Ricotta Mold

Follow the first part of the Ricotta Ribbon Mold recipe through the vigorous beating of the ricotta cheese mixture and the gelatin. Instead of dividing into thirds add 1½ cups of cranberry sauce to the entire mixture and beat thoroughly. Spoon into a mold and refrigerate.

## Pineapple Ricotta Mold

Proceed as for Cranberry Ricotta mold, substituting 1½ cups of drained crushed pineapple for the cranberry sauce.

## Strawberry Mousse

2 cups crushed strawberries
⅓ cup fructose
2 tbsps. lemon juice
1 envelope gelatin
1 tbsp. fructose
¼ cup water
2 egg yolks
½ cup milk
1 tsp. vanilla

Combine the strawberries, fructose and lemon juice. Let stand in refrigerator for several hours or overnight. Add the gelatin and fructose to the ¼ cup cold water. Combine the egg yolks and milk in the top of a double boiler. Stir in the softened gelatin mixture. Cook over hot water, stirring constantly, until the gelatin is dissolved. Let cool until syrupy. Stir in the strawberry mixture and vanilla. Turn into a mold and refrigerate until set. This can be served plain or with whipped cream or ice cream. It also makes a good pie filling and is excellent in a Fructose French Meringue (see recipe).

# Puddings

## Apple-Cottage Cheese Pudding

4 cups apple slices
1 tbsp. lemon or lime juice
1 tbsp. margarine
½ cup fructose
2 tbsps. flour
¼ tsp. salt
1 cup dry curd cottage cheese
1 egg, beaten
1 tsp. cinnamon
½ tsp. ground cloves
2 tbsps. grated coconut, optional (or nuts)

Cook together over low heat the apple slices, juice and margarine for 7 minutes. Let cool to lukewarm. Meanwhile, stir together the fructose, flour and salt. Cream the egg into the cottage cheese and add to this the dry mixture and spices. Combine with the apple slice mixture, stir thoroughly and turn into a greased baking dish. Sprinkle the top evenly with the grated coconut or nuts, if used. Bake at 400 degrees for 20 minutes. This is good served warm, but can be served cold, plain or with whipped cream, sour cream or any of the flavored yogurts (see recipes for Flavored Yogurts). I have found it to be an excellent filling for crepes. It can also be used as a pie filling and goes well with Coconut Cookie Crust (see recipe). 6 to 8 servings.

## Basic Baked Custard

2 eggs
1½ cups milk, scalded and cooled to tepid
2 tbsps. fructose
1 tsp. vanilla or other flavoring

Beat the eggs thoroughly. Pour the milk in slowly as you continue beating. Add the fructose and vanilla and continue beating until well-mixed. Place into 4 well-greased custard cups and place the cups in a pan of hot water up to the level of the custard in the cups. Bake at 325 degrees until a knife inserted comes out clean, about 30 to 40 minutes. Makes 4 servings.

## Basic Baked Custard
## adapted to fructose syrup

1½ cups milk scalded and cooled to tepid
1½ tbsps. 90% fructose syrup
2 eggs
1 tsp. vanilla

Stir the milk and fructose syrup together. Beat the eggs thoroughly and slowly pour the milk into the beaten eggs as you continue beating. Stir in the vanilla. Divide between 4 well-greased custard cups. Place the filled cups in a pan of hot water up to the level of the custard in the cups. Bake at 325 degrees for about an hour.

This makes a soft custard which is very good over fresh or stewed fruits. For a firmer custard use 3 eggs and 2 tbsps. fructose syrup. Makes 4 servings.

Puddings

111

Variations
### Spanish Flan

Spread 2 tbsps. of hot caramelized fructose syrup in each custard cup. Add the custard and bake as directed. Invert into 4 sauce dishes immediately upon removing from oven.

### Fruited Custard

Place 1 tbsp. of soft-dried fruits chopped up, such as apricots, raisins, currants, prunes, etc. or any combination of these, in the bottom of custard cups and add custard.

### Cake Custard

Pour custard over chunks of cake in a greased casserole and bake at 325 degrees until knife comes out clean.

### Coconut Custard

Add ⅓ cup shredded coconut to the Basic Baked Custard batter and bake as directed.

### Creamed Tofu Custard

2 eggs
1⅓ cups tofu
¼ cup fructose
1 tsp. vanilla flavoring, or flavoring of your choice
    (maple, almond, rum; all are good)
½ cup milk, scalded and cooled to tepid

Whisk the eggs and tofu together in a blender until smooth. Add the fructose and vanilla. Slowly add the milk while continuing to blend. Divide among 6 greased custard cups. Set the cups in a pan of hot water that reaches the level of the custard. Bake at 325 degrees 30 to 35 minutes until a table knife comes out clean. Serves 6.

## Chestnut and Cranberry Pudding

1 cup cranberries, sliced in two
2 tbsps. fructose
½ cup diced chestnuts
½ cup bread crumbs
½ cup milk
2 tbsps. margarine
¼ cup fructose
1 egg
½ cup yogurt
½ cup whole wheat flour
¼ tsp. salt
½ tsp. baking soda
¼ tsp. ginger
¼ tsp. allspice
1 recipe cranberry glaze

In a greased casserole combine the cranberries, 2 tbsps. fructose and diced chestnuts. Add the bread crumbs and milk. Let soak while preparing the second mixture. In a bowl cream together the margarine and ¼ cup fructose. Beat in the egg and yogurt. Sift together the remaining dry ingredients and beat in with the mixture in the bowl. Pour the mixture from the bowl into the casserole and stir to combine thoroughly. Bake covered at 350 degrees for 45 minutes. Remove from oven and spread with Cranberry Glaze (see recipe). Return to oven and bake for another 15 minutes or more, until a knife stuck in pudding comes out clean.

## Dutch Carrot Pudding

½ cup grated carrots
½ cup grated potatoes
½ cup sliced apples
¼ cup raisins
¼ cup almonds, sliced (or other nuts)
2 tbsps. melted margarine or butter
½ cup fructose
1 egg, separated
½ cup whole wheat flour
¼ tsp. nutmeg
½ tsp. vanilla

Stir together the carrots, potatoes, apples, raisins and almonds. Cream together the margarine and fructose. Add the egg yolk and mix well. Stir in the first mixture. Then add the whole wheat flour, nutmeg and vanilla. Beat well. The liquid from the potatoes should be sufficient to make this a thick batter. Beat the egg white until fluffy. Fold into the batter. Pour into 1½ pint casserole. Bake at 325 degrees until toothpick comes out clean, about 1 hour and 15 minutes. If placed in a glass oblong dish about 10 inches by 7 inches, it will bake in less time.

This is good served with whipped cream, whipped powdered milk, sour cream or yogurt. When I make it, I like to have leftovers for breakfast served with a generous amount of yogurt. Makes about 6 servings.

## Dutch Carrot Pudding adapted to fructose syrup

2 tbsps. melted margarine or butter
⅓ cup 90% fructose syrup
1 egg, separated
½ cup grated carrots
½ cup grated potatoes
½ cup sliced apples
¼ cup raisins
¼ cup sliced almonds
½ cup whole wheat flour
¼ tsp. nutmeg
½ tsp. vanilla

Stir together the melted shortening and fructose syrup. When this mixture is cooled to lukewarm, stir in the egg yolk. Combine the carrots, potatoes, apples, raisins and almonds. Stir this into the first mixture and continue as in the above recipe. Makes about 6 servings.

## Fruited Corn Meal Pudding

2 cups milk
¼ cup corn meal
2 tbsps. margarine or butter
¼ cup fructose
¼ tsp. salt
½ tsp. ginger
2 eggs, beaten
2 cups sliced fruit (apples, pears, plums, peaches
  or a combination of fresh fruits)
¼ cup dried currants

Bring milk to boil in top of double boiler. Place over hot water and stir in the corn meal. Cook 15 minutes over boiling water, stirring occasionally. Remove from heat and add margarine. Cool slightly and stir in the next 4 ingredients until well-blended. Mix in the fruits and place in buttered casserole. Bake at 325 degrees until toothpick comes out clean, 1 to 1½ hours, depending on juiciness of fruit. Serves 4.

## Noodle Kugel with Apples

Two cups noodles, cooked and drained
2 eggs
¼ cup fructose
¼ cup orange juice
1 tbsp. grated orange rind
¼ cup plain yogurt
¼ cup raisins
1 tsp. cinnamon
2 cups thinly sliced baking apples

Line a greased 6-cup casserole with a thin layer of noodles. Beat the eggs thoroughly with fructose. Beat in the orange juice, rind, cinnamon and yogurt. Fold in the raisins, apple slices and remaining noodles. Spoon into the casserole and bake, uncovered, at 375 degrees until lightly browned, about 35 to 45 minutes.

Puddings

115

## Pineapple Bran-Apple Betty

3 cups soft bread crumbs
2 tbsps. wheat germ
2 tbsps. bran
2 tbsps. butter or margarine
1 cup crushed pineapple
3 cups sliced apples
1 tbsp. lemon juice
⅔ cup pineapple juice
½ tsp. cinnamon
½ tsp. ground cloves
½ tsp. ground allspice
½ cup fructose

Heat the bread crumbs, wheat germ, bran and butter in a large skillet just until the bread crumbs are lightly browned, not dry. Sprinkle the lemon juice over the apples. Combine the fructose and the spices, mixing thoroughly. Layer the ingredients in a greased casserole as follows: On the bottom, one ⅓ of the bread crumb mixture, then ½ of the crushed pineapple, then ½ of the apples, then sprinkle evenly with ½ the spice and fructose mixture, then another ⅓ of the bread crumb mixture, sprinkle with ½ the pineapple juice, then the other ½ of the crushed pineapple, the rest of the apples, the rest of the spice and fructose, the last of the bread crumb mixture, and finally sprinkle with the remaining pineapple juice. Bake at 350 degrees, 40 to 50 minutes.

## Rice Kugel

To capture the schmaltzy flavor I remember from my childhood, you should use chicken fat in this recipe. This is obtained easily by rendering fat from chicken or skimming the top off chilled cooked chicken drippings.

½ cup uncooked rice
1½ cup water
¼ tsp. salt
2 tbsps. chicken fat or other shortening
¼ cup fructose
2 eggs
½ tsp. cinnamon
¼ tsp. nutmeg
¼ tsp. vanilla
½ cup raisins

In a sauce pan bring the rice, salt and water to a boil. Simmer for 10 minutes. Drain and let cool to luke warm. Meanwhile, cream the shortening and fructose. Beat in the eggs. Stir in the seasonings, raisins and rice. Place in a greased casserole. Bake at 350 degrees until lightly browned, 40 to 60 minutes. 6 to 8 servings.

## Traditional Bread Pudding

1 cup diced stale bread
1½ cups milk, scalded
1 egg
¼ cup fructose
¼ tsp. salt
¼ tsp. cinnamon
¼ tsp. cloves
¼ cup raisins

Soak the bread cubes in ¾ cup of the scalded milk. Beat the egg with the fructose. Stir in the remaining milk. Combine thoroughly with the salt cinnamon, cloves and raisins. Add to the soaked bread and mix thoroughly. Turn into a greased 3 or 4 cup casserole. Place the casserole, uncovered, in a pan of hot water and bake in a 350-degree oven until firm, about 1¼ hours. Makes 4 servings.

## Zabaglione

6 egg yolks
¼ cup fructose
½ cup Marsala wine or other natural
   unsweetened fruit juice

Beat the egg yolks with the fructose until creamy. Stir in the wine or juice. Cook over hot water stirring constantly until desired thickness. This versatile, Italian standby, makes good use of leftover egg yolks. It can be served simply in dessert glasses with whipped cream, yogurt or ice cream. It can also be used as a pudding topping. Makes 4 servings.

Puddings

# Fruits, Plain
## and Fancy

## Banana Pineapple Sandwich

1 medium banana
6 pineapple chunks
1 tsp. margarine or butter
1 tsp. fructose
1 tbsp. pineapple juice
1 tbsp. sliced almonds,
    optional

Slice the banana lengthwise and, using toothpicks, attach the pineapple chunks between the banana slices. Melt the margarine in a 5-inch heavy iron skillet. Add the fructose and pineapple juice and heat over a low flame just until the fructose is dissolved. Cut the banana crosswise to fit skillet and turn to coat the banana sandwich. Sprinkle with sliced almonds, if desired. Bake at 400 degrees until banana is tender, approximately 25 minutes. After 15 minutes baste the banana with the pan juices. This recipe, intended for 1 serving, adjusts very well to larger amounts. Simply increase the ingredients proportionately and choose a baking dish to fit. Serve with the pan juices. I like to top this with a dollop of yogurt.

## Cranberry Juice

1 lb. cranberries
6 cups water
⅔ cup fructose

Bring cranberries and water to a boil in a large saucepan. Simmer until cranberries pop, about 5 minutes. Strain and return juice to saucepan. Add the fructose and bring to a boil. Remove from heat. Makes 12 servings.

## Fructose Cranberry Sauce

1 lb. cranberries
1 cup water
1 cup fructose

Place cranberries and water in a saucepan. Cover and bring to a boil. Simmer until cranberries begin to pop. Add the fructose and continue cooking until all of the cranberries have popped.

Fruits, Plain and Fancy

**119**

## Fructose Cranberry Sauce
### adapted to fructose syrup

4 cups cranberries (1 lb.)
½ cup water
⅔ cup 90% fructose syrup

Bring the cranberries and water to a boil and simmer until the cranberries begin to pop. Add the fructose syrup and continue cooking until all of the cranberries have popped. Cranberries sometimes vary in the time it takes for them to pop, depending on such factors as whether or not they have been frozen or their ripeness when picked. It may be necessary to squash a few with a spoon if they have not popped by the time the sauce is the thickness you like.

## Banana Tropicale

4 medium bananas
2 tbsps. fructose
½ tsp. cinnamon
½ tsp. ground cloves
½ tsp. grated nutmeg
⅓ cup unsweetened pineapple juice
2 tbsps. lemon juice
2 tbsps. sliced almonds

Set oven temperature at 350 degrees. Slice bananas in ½ lengthwise. Combine the lemon and pineapple juices with the spices and fructose. Lay the bananas in a shallow, buttered baking dish. Spoon the liquid mixture over the bananas evenly and sprinkle over the top with the sliced almonds. Bake for 20 minutes. Good served with yogurt, whipped cream, ice cream or simply in its own juices. Makes 4 servings.

## Banana Tropicale
## adapted to fructose syrup

4 medium bananas
4 tsps. 90% fructose syrup
½ tsp. cinnamon
½ tsp. ground cloves
½ tsp. grated nutmeg
⅓ cup unsweetened pineapple juice
2 tbsps. lemon juice
2 tbsps. sliced almonds

Slice the bananas in half lengthwise and place side by side in a shallow baking dish. Combine the syrup, spices and juices. Spoon this mixture over the bananas and sprinkle the sliced almonds on top. Bake at 350 degrees until bubbling, about 20 minutes. Serve with yogurt, whipping cream, ice cream or simply in its own juices. Makes 4 servings.

Fruits, Plain and Fancy

## Hawaiian Fruit Barrel

Amounts of ingredients in this recipe are proportional and depend on the size of pineapple you select.

2 cups pineapple cubes from 1 pineapple
1½ cups diced fresh fruit in season. Suggested fruits: peaches; papaya; strawberries; banana; berries; apricots; oranges
¼ cup fructose, more or less depending on tartness of fruits
¼ cup flavoring liquid such as cranberry juice, lemon juice, orange juice or rum

Slice the top off the pineapple saving it to use as a lid. Carefully remove the pulp from the pineapple leaving about ¼ inch layer to keep the shape of the pineapple. Discard the hard core and cut the remainder into cubes, sprinkle the cubes with fructose, 1 tbsp. for each cup. Sprinkle the remaining fructose over the other diced fruits, adjusting amount to the sweetness or tartness of the fruits. Combine the fruits and sprinkle with the flavoring liquid. Chill shell and fruits until ready to serve. Remove from refrigerator and pack the fruit into the pineapple shell. I like to serve this with bowls of Flavored Yogurt (see recipes). Whipped cream may also be used.

## Scandinavian Fruit Compote

2 cups dried fruit combination of your choice,
such as pear, apple, raisins, currants, apricots,
peaches, pineapple, prunes
1 cup cranberry juice
2 cups water
¼ tsp. salt
¼ cup thin lemon slices
½ cup fructose (Since fruits vary in sweetness
   you may want to adjust this)
2 tbsps. minute tapioca

Cook the dried fruits, juice, water, salt and lemon slices until the fruits are tender. Add the fructose and tapioca and cook until the tapioca is clear, about 8 minutes.

## Spiced Scandinavian Fruit Compote

To the above recipe add:
½ tsp. cinnamon
¼ tsp. nutmeg
¼ tsp. ground cloves

## Stuffed Baked Pears

6 medium pears
4 tbsps. raisins
2 tbsps. sliced almonds
2 tbsps. fructose
2 tbsps. butter or margarine
2 tbsps. water
2 tbsps. lemon juice

Peel the pears. Slice in ½ lengthwise and remove stems and cores. Fill the hollows with raisins and almonds. Combine the fructose, butter, water and lemon juice in a small sauce pan and bring to a boil. Place the pears in a baking dish that has been greased and floured. Spoon the hot liquid over them evenly cover and bake at 350 degrees for 45 minutes.

Fruits, Plain and Fancy

## Ginger Baked Pears

Ginger and pears go well together. Follow the above recipe omitting the lemon juice, using 3 tbsps. of water instead of 2 and adding ½ to 1 tsp. of ginger depending on how spicy you like your pears.

## Stuffed Prunes

½ cup cream or Neufchatel cheese
¼ cup fructose jam or cranberry sauce
¼ cup chopped nuts or grated coconut
about 30 medium pitted prunes, moist pack

Combine thoroughly the cheese, jam or cranberry sauce and chopped nuts or coconut. Using a very small spoon, fill the cavities of the prunes. The number will depend on the size of the prunes and how full you like to stuff them. Chill before serving.

## Stuffed Dates

The above stuffing is also delicious with pitted dates.

## Swiss Baked Fruit

1 good sized piece of fruit, cut in ½-inch slices,
  about 1 cup (pear, apple, plums, pineapple,
  etc.)
2 tsps. fructose
2 tbsps. lemon juice; if fruit is tart, you may
  prefer apple or orange juice
¼ cup grated Swiss cheese

Place the fruit in the bottom of a greased baking dish in one layer. Combine the fructose and juice and sprinkle evenly over the fruit. Top with a layer of grated Swiss cheese. Bake at 375 degrees until fruit is bubbly and cheese melted, about 20 minutes.

This is wonderful winter fare in front of a fireplace; and if you are in a festive mood you may substitute your favorite liqueur for the juice. Creme de Menthe is very nice with pears. Increase proportionally for more servings and use an appropriate baking dish.

## Swiss Baked Fruit
## adapted to fructose syrup

For each serving:
1 cup fruit in ½-inch slices
1¼ tsps. 90% fructose syrup
2 tbsps. lemon juice; if fruit is tart you may prefer
  apple or orange juice
¼ cup grated Swiss cheese

Follow the directions for Swiss Baked Fruit above, simply combining fructose syrup, instead of granular fructose, with the lemon juice.

# Preserves and Syrups

## Apple Butter

1 quart chopped apples from apples that have
   been peeled and cored
2 tbsps. apple cider vinegar
2 tbsps. water
1 cup fructose, more or less depending on tartness of apples

Bring the apples, vinegar and water to a boil and simmer until the apples are tender. Press apple pulp with its juice through a coarse sieve and return to sauce pan. Add the fructose and simmer, stirring occasionally, until desired thickness. This makes about 1 pint of apple butter.

## Spiced Apple Butter

To the above recipe add:
½ tsp. cinnamon
¼ tsp. nutmeg
½ tsp. allspice
¼ tsp. ground cloves

## Carrot-Apple Preserves

1½ cups diced carrots
2½ cups diced apples
2 tbsps. lemon juice
1 cup fructose
⅓ cup raisins
½ tsp. ground ginger
½ tsp. ground nutmeg

Steam the carrots for 10 minutes. Place the apples and lemon juice in a sauce pan and simmer over low heat for 10 minutes. Add the remaining ingredients and simmer until desired thickness. Place in sterilized jars. Makes about 2½ cups.

## Berrypicker's Spiced Preserves

4 cups berries, such as blackberries, elderberries, raspberries
2½ cups fructose
¼ cup lemon juice
½ tsp. ground cloves
½ tsp. ground cinnamon
½ tsp. ground allspice

Remove berries from stems and wash. Place in a sauce pan and bring to a boil over low heat, stirring occasionally to prevent scorching. Let simmer for 5 minutes. Add the fructose, lemon juice and spices. Cook until desired thickness. I like this as a syrup for puddings, ice cream and pancakes. You may prefer a thicker consistency for spreading on bread. Place in sterilized jar. Makes about 1 pint.

## Grape-Apple Preserves

6 cups grapes, washed and stemmed
¼ cup apple cider vinegar
2 cups fructose
2 cups apple slices

Slice grapes and remove seeds. Place in a stainless sauce pan with vinegar and fructose over medium heat. Bring to a boil. Add the apple slices and continue cooking, stirring occasionally to avoid scorching, until desired thickness. Ladle into sterilized jars. Makes about 1 quart.

## Fig and Pineapple Preserves

2 cups dried figs, chopped
1 cup canned crushed pineapple
1 cup pineapple juice
1 cup water
1 cup fructose
2 tbsps. lemon juice

Remove stems from figs and chop into pieces about ¼ inch. Combine with the rest of the ingredients and let stand for 2 to 3 hours. Bring to boil over low heat and simmer to desired thickness, about 20 minutes, stirring occasionally to prevent scorching. Place in sterilized jars. This makes about 1 quart.

## Spicy Grape-Apple Preserves

To the above recipe add with the apple slices:
¼ tsp. nutmeg
½ tsp. cinnamon
½ tsp. cloves

## Spiced Fig and Pineapple Preserves

To the above ingredients add:
1 tsp. ground ginger
½ tsp. nutmeg
½ tsp. cinnamon

Preserves and Syrups

129

## Loquat Jam

The loquat is a small, round yellow fruit growing in clusters on a broad-leafed tropical and semi-tropical tree, bearing fruit in May or June. This is one of the most delicious of fruits and since the season is short, it is especially desirable to preserve them.

3 cups loquat chunks
1 cup fructose
¼ cup lemon juice

Wash loquats. Remove stem, blossom ends and seeds. Cut into very small pieces, about ¼ inch thick and wide. Measure 3 cups of these pieces. Place with fructose and lemon juice in a sauce pan. Bring to a boil and cook to desired thickness. Makes about 1 pint loquat jam.

## Pear Marmalade

1 quart chopped pears from pears which have been washed, stemmed and cored
3 medium or 2 large oranges (enough to make 2 cups of orange chunks)
2 cups fructose
2 tbsps. cider vinegar

Place the unpeeled oranges in a bowl and cover with boiling hot water. Let stand overnight or for 8 hours. Slice the oranges thin and then quarter the slices to make approximately 2 cups. Place the oranges, pears and vinegar in a sauce pan and bring to a boil over medium heat. Add the fructose and simmer until thick and syrupy. Ladle into sterilized jars. Makes about 3 cups.

## Plum Jam

plums
fructose
lemon juice, optional

Wash plums and remove pits. Simmer in a stainless steel or enameled pot until tender. Force through a coarse strainer and measure. For each cup of plum pulp, add ½ cup of fructose and, if you like, 2 tsps. lemon juice. Cook until thick on low heat, stirring frequently to prevent scorching. Store in sterilized jars. Allow to cool before sealing.

## Sweet Bell Pepper and Lime Marmalade

3 cups chopped red bell pepper
1 lime sliced thin, about ½ cup
½ tsp. salt
1 cup cider vinegar
2 cups fructose

Prepare the red bell pepper by cutting in ½ and removing stem, seeds and membrane. Chop the pepper and measure 3 cups. Do not discard the liquid which is pressed out by the chopping especially if you use a blender. Place in a sauce pan the chopped peppers with their liquid, the lime slices, salt and vinegar. Bring to a boil and cook over low heat until the rind of the lime is tender, about ½ hour. Add the fructose and cook until the marmalade is thick. Place in a sterilized jar and cover. Makes about 2 cups.

## Rum Syrup

½ cup water
½ cup fructose
¼ cup rum

Bring to a boil the fructose and water. Let simmer 3 to 10 minutes depending on the use to which you will put the syrup. Stir in the rum and bring to a boil once more. Rum syrup is traditional with babas or savarins. When so used, the syrup should be quite thin so that it will better permeate the cakes. Makes ⅔ cup.

## Caramelized Fructose Syrup

1 cup fructose
⅓ cup boiling water
flavoring, optional

Melt the fructose in a heavy skillet over low heat stirring constantly until it begins to froth and turns golden. Remove from heat and stir in the boiling water adding it **very slowly**. This makes a little more than ¾ cup of syrup. With its distinctive almost honey-like caramel flavor, it is delicious on crepes or cakes that have been pricked and basic to caramel cake and flan. If you wish, you may add flavorings such as ½ tsp. maple flavoring or almond extract or ¼ cup rum.

## Lemon Syrup

1 cup fructose
½ cup water
2 tbsps. lemon juice

In a small heavy pan heat the fructose over low heat until melted and golden. Slowly add water and continue heating, simmering for 10 minutes. Stir in the lemon juice and remove from heat. Lemon syrup is traditional for Greek recipes such as Baklava (see recipe) and also makes a good cake topping.


## Lemon Syrup adapted to fructose syrup

⅔ cup 90% fructose syrup
¼ cup water
2 tbsps. lemon juice

In a small sauce pan heat the syrup and water together, bringing to a boil. Simmer until syrupy thick, about 210 degrees on a candy thermometer. Stir in the lemon juice. Store in a covered bottle or small jar.


## Natural Apple Syrup

1 pint unfiltered, unsweetened apple juice
2 tbsps. cider vinegar
2 cups fructose

Combine ingredients and bring to a boil over medium heat. Continue cooking until syrupy, about 220 degrees on a candy thermometer. Store in covered bottle or jar. Makes approximately 1 pint.

Sweets Without Guilt

## Natural Apple Syrup
### adapted to fructose syrup

3 cups unfiltered, unsweetened apple juice
2 tbsps. cider vinegar
2 cups 90% fructose syrup

Combine the ingredients in a sauce pan and bring to a boil over medium heat. Continue cooking until syrupy, about 220 degrees on a candy thermometer. If you do not have a thermometer, be sure to take into account the fact that the syrup will thicken as it cools. Store in a covered bottle or jar. Makes about 1 quart.

## Spiced Apple Syrup

To the above recipe add ½ tsp. cinnamon, ¼ tsp. ground cloves and a dash of nutmeg. Cook as directed.

## Orange Syrup

1 cup fructose
⅓ cup water
⅓ cup orange juice

Place the fructose in a small, heavy pan over low heat until it is melted and golden. Add enough orange juice to the water to bring it up to ½ cup. Add this slowly to the fructose and simmer for 10 minutes. Add the remaining orange juice and remove from heat.

# Candies and Confections

## Ambrosia Caramels

1 cup fructose
¼ cup chopped unsweetened dried pineapple
¼ cup Chopped Candied Orange Peel (see
   recipe)
¼ cup grated coconut
¼ cup chopped dried banana chips
¼ cup sliced almonds
½ tsp. ginger
About 3 tbsps. coconut for coating
1 tbsp. lemon juice

Combine in a bowl the pineapple, orange peel, coconut ¼ cup, banana chips, sliced almonds and ginger. In a heavy small skillet heat the fructose, stirring, until it is golden and bubbly. Turn off heat and stir in the lemon juice. Pour over the mixture in bowl and stir together quickly and thoroughly. Form into balls approximately ¾ inch in diameter and roll in the coconut. It may be necessary to reheat the caramel mixture over hot water for the last few balls. Store in an airtight jar. Makes about 2 dozen.

## Candied Orange Peel

The ingredients in this recipe are proportional.

Oranges
Water
Salt
Lemon or lime juice
Fructose

Scrub oranges with a soft brush. Score lengthwise with a knife so that the peel will come off in quarter segments. Place in salted water, 1 teaspoon salt to 2 cups water, and cover the orange peel with weights. Jars filled with water may be used as weights. Let stand overnight or at least 5 hours. Pour off the salted water and rinse the orange peel. Remove as much as possible of the white membrane. Cut into strips approx- imately ¼-inch wide. Place in sauce pan and cover with water. Bring to a boil and drain. Repeat. For each cup of orange peel strips put ¾ cup fructose, ¼ cup water and 1 tbsp. lime or lemon juice in a heavy sauce pan. Add the drain- ed orange peel and cook over very low heat, turn- ing the peels frequently, until most of the syrup is absorbed and there is very little left in the bottom of the sauce pan. Remove the peels with a slotted spoon and place on a wire rack. Because fructose absorbs water from the air, it is essential that the peels be rolled in something other than fructose. Among good coatings are unsweetened grated coconut, ground almonds, carob powder mixed with spices to taste, ground sesame seeds, bran, wheat germ. Candied orange peels should be stored, after coating, in covered jars.

## Carob-Caramel Fudge

2 cups fructose
1½ cups unflavored yogurt
½ cup powdered carob
1 tbsp. margarine
1 tbsp. instant coffee
¼ tsp. baking soda
¾ cup chopped nuts

Place the fructose in a heavy skillet and heat until it melts into a clear golden liquid, stirring frequently. Meanwhile combine the yogurt, powdered carob and instant coffee in a sauce pan and bring to a boil. Slowly stir the fructose into the sauce pan mixture and cook, stirring frequently, to the soft ball stage, 240 degrees on a candy thermometer. Remove from heat and stir in the baking soda and margarine. Add ½ cup of the nuts and continue beating until very thick and cool enough to handle. With buttered fingers shape into balls about ¾ of an inch in diameter. Roll the balls to coat them in the remaining nuts. If you wish to store, layer them with foil. Makes about 40 pieces.

## Carrot Balls

This is an adaptation of a traditional Passover recipe.

1 cup carrots, steamed and mashed
¼ cup orange juice
¾ cup fructose
½ tsp. ginger
¼ cup ground sesame seeds
1 tbsp. margarine or butter
⅓ cup grated coconut

Combine mashed carrots, orange juice, fructose and ginger in a sauce pan. Cook over low heat until the mixture is thick and all the syrup is absorbed, stirring occasionally to prevent scorching. Add the margarine and sesame seed and beat thoroughly until the mixture is cool enough to handle. Form into balls approximately 1 inch in diameter and roll in the grated coconut. If not used immediately, place in an air-tight container and store in refrigerator. Makes about 2 dozen balls.

Candies and Confections

**137**

## Divinity Fructose

1 cup fructose
1/8 tsp. salt
¼ cup water
1 tsp. vanilla
1 egg white
½ cup chopped nuts
⅓ cup ground nuts

Bring to a boil in a heavy sauce pan, the fructose, salt and water. Cook over low heat until the syrup reaches a little past the hard ball stage, about 260 degrees on the candy thermometer. In the meantime beat egg white until stiff. As you continue beating, slowly add the syrup to the egg white. Then add vanilla. Continue beating until the mixture is thick and holds its shape. Fold in the chopped nuts. Push 1 teaspoonful at a time into the ground nuts and, using two spoons, roll to form evenly coated balls. This makes about 3 dozen balls. However, if you are involved in a diet which requires that you measure your fructose by teaspoons, you may want to make them slightly smaller to make 4 dozen, as there are 48 tsps. in a cup of fructose. Store in a tightly closed container, in refrigerator or, for longer time, in your freezer. Put waxed paper between layers.

## Coconut Divine

Follow the above recipe, substituting coconut for the ground and chopped nuts.

## Glazed Nuts

1 cup nuts of your choice
1 cup fructose
¼ tsp. salt
½ tsp. maple flavoring

Place nuts loosely on a pan in a 375-degree oven. Meanwhile cook the fructose in a small, heavy iron pan (mine is 6 inches), stirring constantly until it is melted to a clear golden color, about 10 minutes. Remove nuts from oven and spread on a greased 8-inch pan or dish. Stir salt and maple flavoring into the syrup and pour evenly over the nuts, turning the nuts quickly so that they will be evenly coated. Let cool and break into pieces. If you have any left to store, layer with foil in a tightly covered container.

## Lime-Coconut Caramels

1 cup fructose
2 tbsps. lime juice
2 tbsps. water
1 cup coconut, grated
2 tbsps. coconut, grated

Combine the liquids and the fructose in a heavy saucepan. Boil until the syrup reaches 260 degrees, the hard ball stage. Remove from heat and stir in 1 cup coconut. Keep stirring until the mixture is thick enough to shape. Push off a rounded half-teaspoon into a small container of the 2 tbsps. coconut. Roll into the coconut shaping into a ball. This makes 24 caramels. If the mixture solidifies to the point of being difficult to work, heat, placing the saucepan over another pan of hot water, double-boiler fashion, until it is soft enough to shape easily.

Candies and Confections

**139**

## Mexican Raisin Nuggets

This is a modification of the concentrated milk and sugar candy called **dulce de leche** which I enjoyed so much in Mexico.

1½ cups fructose
¼ cup water
1 cup skimmed milk powder
¼ cup chopped raisins
½ tsp. cinnamon
¼ tsp. cardamon
¼ tsp. ground cloves
1 tbsp. butter or margarine
3 tbsps. bran

In a heavy skillet heat the fructose until melted and golden. Stir in the water. Mix together in a sauce pan the milk powder, raisins and spices. Pour the fructose and water mixture over this and heat, stirring constantly, until the candy forms a firm ball when a small amount is dropped in cold water. Beat in the margarine and let cool slightly. Shape into balls about ¾ inch in diameter. Roll in the bran. Store between layers of plastic wrap in an air-tight container. Makes about 30 nuggets.

## Mexican Raisin Nuggets adapted to fructose syrup

1 cup 90% fructose syrup
1 cup skimmed milk powder
½ tsp. cinnamon
¼ tsp. cardamon
¼ tsp. ground cloves
¼ cup chopped raisins
1 tbsp. butter or margarine
3 tbsps. bran

In a sauce pan over a low fire heat the syrup until bubbly. Add the milk powder and spices and continue cooking, stirring to prevent scorching until a small amount forms a firm ball when dropped in cold water. Beat in the raisins and margarine. Let cool slightly. Shape into balls about ¾ of an inch in diameter. Roll these in the bran. Store these between layers of plastic wrapping in an air tight container. Makes about 30 nuggets.

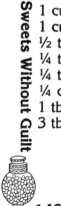

## Popcorn Balls

⅓ cup water
1 tsp. butter or margarine
½ tsp. apple cider vinegar
1 cup fructose
6 cups popped corn

Heat the water and butter in a small saucepan until the butter is melted. Add the vinegar and fructose and cook covered over low heat for 5 minutes. Remove cover and continue cooking over low heat until just a little past the soft ball stage, 260 degrees on a candy thermometer. While this is cooking heat the popped corn in a warm oven, about 250 degrees. Pour the syrup over the corn and mix thoroughly with a wooden spoon. Spread compactly in a buttered dish to cool. When cool enough to handle, form into balls approximately 2 inches in diameter using your buttered fingers. Wrap in clear plastic. Makes about 2 dozen. These make effective holiday ornaments.

## Popcorn-Raisin Balls

Following the above recipe, stir ½ cup chopped raisins into the popped corn. Then combine with the syrup. Makes 2½ dozen.

## Popcorn-Peanut Balls

Following the recipe for popcorn balls, add a cup of chopped peanuts before combining with the syrup. Makes about 34 balls.

Candies and Confections

141

## Sesame Seed Candy

3 tbsps. margarine
¾ cup fructose
1/8 tsp. salt
¼ tsp. baking soda
¾ cup sesame seeds

Combine the margarine, fructose and salt in a heavy 7-inch skillet and heat until it begins to bubble. Add the baking soda and the sesame seeds. Continue cooking, stirring from time to time, until the hard crack stage or 290 to 300 degrees on a candy thermometer. Spread into a greased 8-inch square pan. When cool enough to hold its shape but still warm, score in squares with a sharp knife. To store, remove from pan and place in a covered jar using plastic wrapping between the layers of squares. Makes about 25 squares.

Chopped nuts of your choice may be substituted for the sesame seeds in this recipe.

## Taffy Chestnuts

1 cup shelled chestnuts
½ cup fructose
2 tbsps. rosy liquid such as Cranberry Juice (see
    recipe) or a dry red wine
1/8 tsp. cream of tartar

To prepare chestnuts: With a sharp knife cut gashes on the flat side of chestnuts. Boil for 10 minutes. Remove shells and skin while chestnuts are hot. It may be necessary to reheat as the shells come off more easily while hot. Steam the shelled chestnuts until a knife penetrates easily, but they should still be firm.

Heat the fructose in a heavy pan, stirring occasionally, until it turns a golden color and begins to bubble. Stir in the cream of tartar and juice. Using a slotted spoon, place chestnuts, a few at a time, in the syrup turning so that they will be coated on all sides. Remove to a buttered plate leaving enough space between chestnuts so that they do not touch. It will probably be necessary to reheat the syrup before you have coated all the chestnuts. The leftover syrup can be used to fill in any thin spots you see on the chestnuts. Store between layers of foil in a tight container.

## Welsh Rarebit Caramels

¾ cup skimmed milk powder
6 tbsps. powdered carob
1/8 tsp. salt
¾ cup grated cheddar cheese
1½ cups fructose
1 tbsp. butter or margarine
1 tsp. vanilla
6 tbsps. chopped nuts

Thoroughly combine the milk powder, carob and salt. Stir in the grated cheddar cheese. In a heavy skillet melt the fructose until clear and beginning to bubble. Turn off heat and immediately add the combined dry ingredients stirring vigorously. Beat in the margarine and vanilla. This should be very thick by now. Stir in the chopped nuts and mix thoroughly. Spread into a well-greased pan or dish 7-inch square or 8 inches by 6 inches. Cut into squares. Makes about 3 dozen pieces.

# Index

Almond and Raisin Upside Down Snails, 15
Almond-Coconut Crust, 71
Almond-Coconut Crust adapted to fructose syrup, 71
Ambrosia Caramels, 135
Angelita Cupcakes, 35
Anise Banana Bars, 50
Apple Butter, 127
Apple-Cottage Cheese Pudding, 110
Apple-Date Cake, 25
Apple-Date Cake adapted to fructose syrup, 25
Apple-Ginger Upside Down Cake, 26
Apple Juice Crepes, 77
Apple Strudel, 80
Apple Yogurt Plum Jam Pie, 86
Baklava, 82
Baklava adapted to fructose syrup, 83
Banana Date-Nut Fiesta Pie, 89
Banana-Date Oatmeal Squares, 51
Banana Pineapple Sandwiches, 119
Banana Tropicale, 120
Banana Tropicale adapted to fructose syrup, 121
Banana Yogurt Cake, 27
Banana Yogurt Cake adapted to fructose syrup, 28
Basic Baked Custard, 111
Basic Baked Custard adapted to fructose syrup, 111
Bean Curd and Pineapple Strudel, 81
Berrypicker's Spiced Preserves, 128
Broiled Caramel Frosting, 39
Broiled Caramel-Nut Frosting, 39
Broiled Coconut-Caramel Frosting, 39
Cake Custard, 112
**Cakes, 24**
California Gold Cheese Dessert, 93
Candied Orange Peel, 136
**Candies and Confections, 134**
Caramel Cake, 28
Caramelized Fructose Syrup, 131
Carob-Caramel Fudge, 137
Carob-Mocha Bavarian Cream, 94
Carob-Mocha Pie, 94
Carob Mocha Yogurt, 97
Carob Mocha Yogurt adapted to fructose syrup, 98
Carrot and Pineapple Cake, 29
Carrot-Apple Preserves, 128
Carrot Balls, 137
Carrot-Coconut Cookies, 67
Cheese and Raisin Topped Coffee Cake, 18
Cheese and Whole Wheat Streusel Topping, 46
Cheese Cake with Marmalade, 32
Cheese Pastry, 70
Cheese Triangles, 70
Chestnut and Cranberry Pudding, 113
Chewy Carob Wafers, 65

Coconut Cookie Crust, 71
Coconut Custard, 112
Coconut Divine, 138
Coconut Lace Cookies, 64
Coffee-Flavored Chiffon Pie, 89
**Cookies, 49**
Corn Meal Ginger Cake, 34
Cottage Cheese Brownies, 56
Cottage Cheese Topping or Filling, 44
Cranberry Glace, 47
Cranberry Juice, 119
Cranberry Ricotta Mold, 108
Cream Cheese Filled Crescents, 16
Cream Cheese Frostings, 41
Cream Cheese Rolled Cookies, 68
Creamed Tofu Custard, 112
Creamy Boiled Frosting, 38
Creamy Orange Boiled Frosting, 38
Creamy Lemon Whip, 106
Crescents, 19
Crumbly Ginger Foundation, 72
Crumbly Ginger Foundation adapted to fructose syrup, 72
Date and Grape-Nut Mousse, 95
Date and Peanut Butter Clusters, 59
Date-Nut Pumpkin Cookies, 60
Delectable Beet Bars, 58
Divinity Fructose, 138
Dutch Carrot Pudding, 114
Dutch Carrot Pudding adapted to fructose syrup, 114
Festive Almond Cookies, 57
Fig and Pineapple Preserves, 129
Filo Cookies, 63
Flavored Yogurts, 97
Fresh Fruit Yogurt, 99
Frosty Grape-Orange Yogurt Pudding, 96
Frosty Grape-Orange Yogurt Pudding adapted to fructose syrup, 97
Frozen Apricot Cream, 99
Frozen Cranberry-Tofu Cream, 100
Frozen Fruit-Nut Custard, 101
Fructose Cranberry Sauce, 119
Fructose Cranberry Sauce adapted to fructose syrup, 120
Fructose French Meringue, 78
Fructose French Meringue Topping, 79
Fructose Syrup Yogurt, 98
Fruited Corn Meal Pudding, 115
Fruited Custard, 112
**Fruits Plain and Fancy, 118**
Gertrude Maynard's Wholesome Tasty Cookies, 61

Gertrude Maynard's Wholesome Tasty Cookies adapted to fructose syrup, 62
Ginger Baked Pears, 124
Glazed Nuts, 139
Grape-Apple Preserves, 129
Hawaiian Fruit Barrel, 122
Hearty Prune-Nut Bread, 22
Kiss With Squeeze Apple Pie, 86
Layered Refrigerator Cake, 102
Lemon Chiffon Pie, 90
Lemon Chiffon Pie adapted to fructose syrup, 90
Lemon-Glazed Peanut Butter Bars, 59
Lemon Meringue Pie, 87
Lemon Spread Glaze, 47
Lemon Syrup, 132
Lemon Syrup adapted to fructose syrup, 132
Lime-Coconut Caramels, 139
Little Brown Babas, 20
Loquat Jam, 130
Mandarin Cream Pie Filling, 103
Mandarin Cream Pie Filling adapted to fructose syrup, 104
Margaret's Apple-Nut Torte, **27**
Meringue Topping, 48
Mexican Raisin Nuggets, 140
Mexican Raisin Nuggets adapted to fructose syrup, 140
Mocha Brownies, 56
Mocha-Milk Topping, 44
Mock Chestnut Chiffon Pie, 91
Multi-Grain Sweet Roll Dough, 14
Natural Apple Syrup, 132
Natural Apple Syrup adapted to fructose syrup, 133
Noodle Kugel with Apples, 115
Nut and Rye Wafer Marguerites, 66
Nut and Rye Wafer Marguerites adapted to fructose syrup, 66
Oatmeal-Buttermilk Sweet Dough, 21
Oatmeal Lace Cookies, 64
Oatmeal Lace Cookies adapted to fructose syrup, 64
Oatmeal Streusel Topping, 45
Old Dutch Spice Cake, 30
Old-Fashion Peanut Butter Cookies, modified, 52
Open Sesame Yam Gems, 67
Orange Chiffon Pie, 91
Orange Custard, 42
Orange Custard adapted to fructose syrup, 43
Orange Custard Pie, 43
Orange Gelatin Cake, 31
Orange Spread Glaze, 47
Orange Syrup, 133
Party Cream Puffs, 76
**Pastries and Foundations, 68**
Peanut Butter Bars, 52
Peanut Butter Cookie Crust, 73
Peanut Butter Jam-wich Cookies, 53
Peanut-Pumpkin Cake, 33
Pear Marmalade, 130

**Pie Fillings, 85**
Pineapple and Chestnut Ice Cream, 105
Pineapple Biscuit Tortoni, 95
Pineapple Bran-Apple Betty, 116
Pineapple Glaze, 48
Pineapple-Plum Yogurt Dessert, 107
Pineapple Ricotta Mold, 108
Pineapple Upside Down Cake, 26
Plum Jam, 130
Plum Swirl Cheese Cake, **33**
Popcorn Balls, 141
Popcorn Peanut Balls, 141
Popcorn Raisin Balls, 141
Potato-Carob Brownies, 53
Potato Coffee Cake, 13
**Preface, 6**
**Preserves and Syrups, 126**
Pretty Pink Frosting, 38
Prune Whip Pie with Chestnuts, 88
**Puddings, 109**
Puffed Cereal Carob Cookies, 58
Pumpkin Apple-Butter Pie, 88
Pumpkin Raisin Loaf, 10
Pumpkin Raisin Loaf adapted to fructose syrup, 11
Raisin Bread Toffee, 12
**Refrigerator Desserts, 92**
Refrigerator Sweet Roll Dough, 17
Refrigerator Sweet Roll Dough adapted to fructose syrup, 18
Rice Flour and Sunflower Seed Pie Crust, **73**
Rice Kugel, 116
Ricotta Ribbon Mold, 107
Rolled Strudel Dough, 79
Rum Syrup, 131
Samovar Tea Cakes, 36
Scandinavian Fruit Compote, 123
Scottish Tea Scones, 36
Sesame Seed Candy, 142
Shredded Wheat and Peanut Crust, 74
Shredded Wheat and Raisin Cookies, 54
Shredded Wheat and Raisin Cookies adapted to fructose syrup, 55
Spanish Flan, 112
Spiced Apple Butter, 127
Spiced Apple Syrup, 133
Spiced Fig and Pineapple Preserves, 129
Spiced Scandinavian Fruit Compote, 123
Spicy Grape-Apple Preserves, 129
Strawberry Mousse, 108
Strawberry Shortcake, 30
Stuffed Baked Pears, 123
Stuffed Dates, 124
Stuffed Prunes, 124
Sweet Bell Pepper and Lime Marmalade, 131
Swiss Baked Fruit, 125
Swiss Baked Fruit adapted to fructose syrup, 125
Taffy Chestnuts, 143
Tipsy Little Angels, 35

**Toppings and Fillings, 37**
Traditional Bread Pudding, 117
Vegetable Oil Pie Crust with Corn Meal, 74
Versatile Coconut Topping, 40
Welsh Rarebit Caramels, 144
Whole Wheat Muerbe Teig, 75
Whole Wheat Streusel Topping, 45
Whole Wheat Streusel Topping adapted to
    fructose syrup, 46
Yeast Dough Cinnamon Cookies, 16
Yeasty Date-Sunflower Seed Bars, 23
**Yeasty Sweets, 9**
Yogurt Banana Pie, 87
Yogurt with Preserves, 98
Yugoslavian Pinwheels, 84
Zabaglione, 117
Zucchini-Carob Cake, 34

# Suppliers of Fructose

If you are unable to obtain fructose from your grocer or health food store, write to one of the following American suppliers:

**Batter-Lite Foods, Inc.**
P.O. Box 341
Beloit, Wisconsin 53511

**Doctor's Choice Fructose**
Thompson Medical Co.
919 Third Avenue
New York, New York 10022

**Estee Corporation**
169 Lackawanna Avenue
Parsippany, New Jersey 07054

**General Nutrition Corporation**
921 Penn Avenue
Pittsburgh, Pennsylvania 15230

Or for your convenience, you may order fructose directly from the publisher in the following quantities:

1 lb. fructose in a pouch . . . . . . . . . . . . . . . . . . . . . . . . . . . . . . . . . . . . . . $5.95
2 lbs. fructose in a reusable canister . . . . . . . . . . . . . . . . . . . . . . . . . . . . . $8.95
5 lbs. fructose in a bag . . . . . . . . . . . . . . . . . . . . . . . . . . . . . . . . . . . . . . . $16.95

All prices include $2.00 postage and handling.

Send your check to:
Fructose/East Woods Press
820 East Boulevard
Charlotte, NC 28203

# The Fructose Cookbook

If you have enjoyed **Sweets Without Guilt** for its delectable dessert recipes using fructose, you will want to get a copy of **The Fructose Cookbook**, Minuha Cannon's bestselling fructose recipe book!

**The Fructose Cookbook** has over 126 recipes, from beverages and soups to vegetables and main courses. Of course they are nutritious and require other healthful ingredients besides fructose. They are also delicious and internationally inspired, just like **Sweets Without Guilt!**

Among the recipes are Mediterranean chicken, Ceviche, Hawaiian lamb patties, chopped herring salad, hearty banana soup, lemon-glazed carrots, zucchini bars, yogurt rolls, rice flour muffins, rye-potato bread, feta cheese pancakes, and coffee liqueur.

**The Fructose Cookbook** will fit right on your shelf with **Sweets Without Guilt** and the two will bring you hundreds of nutritious meals.

$5.95 at your bookseller
or from the publisher:
The East Woods Press
820 East Boulevard
Charlotte, NC 28203

# About the Author

Minuha Cannon is a free-lance writer living in Richmond, California. She is a former piano instructor and teacher of mentally handicapped children. Besides cooking and writing, she enjoys painting, playing the concertina or folk dancing.

Minu's bestseller, **The Fructose Cookbook**, (1979, East Woods Press), has gone back to press four times as of this writing. Minu's knowledge of the benefits of fructose grew out of her interest in biochemistry. After several years of experimenting with fructose in her own collection of unusual, wholesome dishes, she was encouraged by friends to have her recipes published.